LANCASTER PAMPHLETS

Elizabeth I and Religion
1558–1603

Susan Doran

London and New York

First published 1994
by Routledge
11 New Fetter Lane, London EC4P 4EE

Simultaneously published in the USA and Canada
by Routledge Inc.
29 West 35th Street, New York, NY 10001

Typeset in 10 on 12 point Bembo by
Ponting–Green Publishing Services, Chesham, Bucks
Printed in Great Britain by
Clays Ltd, St Ives plc

British Library Cataloguing in Publication Data
A catalogue record for this book is available from the British Library

Library of Congress Cataloging in Publication Data
Doran, Susan
Elizabeth I and religion, 1558–1603 / Susan Doran
p.   cm. – (Lancaster pamphlets)
Includes bibliographical references
1. Elizabeth I, Queen of England, 1533–1603.
2. Reformation–England.
3. England–Church history–16th century.
4. England–Church history–17th century.
5. Great Britain–History–Elizabeth I, 1558–1603.
I. Title.   II. Series.
BR756.D665   1994
274.2'06–dc20   93–19320

ISBN 0–415–07352–9

For my family and my students

Contents

Foreword

Lancaster Pamphlets offer concise and up-to-date accounts of major historical topics, primarily for the help of students preparing for Advanced Level examinations, though they should also be of value to those pursuing introductory courses in universities and other institutions of higher education. Without being all-embracing, their aims are to bring some of the central themes or problems confronting students and teachers into sharper focus than the textbook writer can hope to do; to provide the reader with some of the results of recent research which the textbook may not embody; and to stimulate thought about the whole interpretation of the topic under discussion.

Time chart

1

Introduction

On the death of Mary I there was a surprisingly smooth transition to the accession of her half-sister Elizabeth. Despite the Catholic view that she had been born out of wedlock, neither the Pope nor Philip II of Spain challenged the new queen's legitimacy and right to rule, and the English Catholics in power made no move to resist her succession by force of arms. None the less most politicians were conscious that the reign of Elizabeth would not be so smooth but on the contrary would bring about major upheavals in religious and political life. As De Feria, the Spanish ambassador, told Philip II soon after Elizabeth's accession: 'things are in such a hurly-burly and confusion that fathers do not know their own children'. Few doubted that Elizabeth, as the daughter of Henry VIII and Anne Boleyn, would rescind England's ties with the Papacy, and some expected her to return the religion of the country to Protestantism.

The marriage of Elizabeth's parents had been the occasion, if not the cause, of the original break with Rome and Henry VIII's declaration of the royal supremacy. By the Act of Supremacy of 1534, parliament had recognized the king's title as Supreme Head of the Church and his power 'to visit, repress, redress, reform, order, correct, restrain and amend all such errors, heresies, abuses, offences, contempts, and enormities, what-soever they be'. For the remainder of the reign, Henry had used

1

his assumed rights to expropriate ecclesiastical property and reform the Church. Church reform under Henry was both tentative and moderate; it was ordered that English bibles be placed in churches, certain 'superstitions' were condemned and the Litany (part of the Morning Prayer) was translated into English. Catholic doctrines, however, remained largely intact. Consequently, in the 1540s men and women were still being burnt as heretics for denying transubstantiation (the Catholic doctrine that the wafer and wine were transformed into the body and blood of Christ after their sanctification by the priest at the mass).

At Henry's court, however, an unofficial reform group continued to have influence. Some members were Protestant, but others are better described as 'evangelicals' as they tended to be orthodox or unclear in their doctrinal views, although they wished to see the removal of 'superstitious' practices and a greater emphasis on the Scriptures. At the death of Henry, members of this reform group seized power, and as a result the reign of Edward VI saw the first stage in the Protestant Reformation of England.

On the Continent the Protestants had splintered into many different confessional groups, each owing allegiance to the doctrines, liturgy and ecclesiastical order devised by its own theologians. The three most important theologians were Luther, Zwingli (who had been killed in 1531 but whose influence continued through his successor at Zurich, Heinrich Bullinger) and Calvin. By the late 1540s, however, the Zwinglians and Calvinists had reached some agreement on a joint confession of faith, while quarrels were developing among the Lutheran theologians, especially after their leader's death in 1546. It is, therefore, most convenient (though a simplification) to talk of two main Protestant confessions: the Lutheran and that of the Swiss Reformed Churches, comprising the Zwinglians and Calvinists. They differed in their doctrines on predestination and the Eucharist, in their liturgy, in their approach to discipline and in the organization of their churches.

On predestination, the Swiss Reformers emphasized double predestination; that is to say they believed that all men and women were predestined by God before their birth either for election (salvation) or reprobation (damnation). They also affirmed that the elect were assured of their salvation even if they lapsed in their moral behaviour, just as the reprobate could never earn salvation by carrying out good deeds.

On the Eucharist, the Swiss Reformers denied the *corporeal* (physical) presence of Christ's body in the bread and wine at the communion service; but while the Zwinglians emphasized the commemorative significance of communion (that the service was essentially a memorial to the Last Supper), the Calvinists spoke of the *spiritual* presence of Christ at communion. Their agreed disbelief in a corporeal presence, however, led all the Swiss Reformers to object to the use of an altar and vestments (the colourful priestly dress), both of which signified the sacrifice of Christ's body in the ceremony of the Eucharist.

Liturgically, the services of the Reformed Church were austere, with ritual kept to a minimum; kneeling, genuflexion and crossings were scorned as superstitious, while organ music and choral singing were thought unnecessary and distracting. Similarly, the interiors of their churches were simple, lacking decoration and colour; since the presence of images was condemned as idolatrous, carvings, sculptures and stained-glass windows were removed and wall-paintings obliterated by whitewash.

Finally, the Swiss Reformers moved away entirely from the hierarchical organization and clerical dominance of the Catholic Church and developed their own system of government, which is known as Presbyterianism. Their local churches were run by a three- or four-fold ministry: pastors chosen by their congregations to preach the Word, lay elders to be responsible for correcting the moral faults of the community, lay deacons to care for the poor and organize parish finances, and in addition doctors to preserve pure doctrine. Representatives were sent from individual congregations to meet in regional and national assemblies, called synods.

England under Edward VI was exposed to both Lutheran and Swiss Reformed influences, but as the reign progressed more and more English theologians came into contact with Swiss Reformed refugees from the Continent, and began to share their vision of a truly reformed Church. Central parts of the first Edwardian Prayer Book of 1549 were more Lutheran in inspiration than Swiss Reformed. Its communion service 'commonly called the mass' expressed belief in the corporeal presence of Christ in the bread and wine, and its rubric on ornaments laid down that vestments should be worn by the minister. Swiss

Reformed theologians residing in England therefore made criticisms of the Prayer Book to Archbishop Cranmer, who incorporated their proposed amendments into a second Prayer Book, authorized by parliament in 1552. The communion service of the Second Edwardian Prayer Book denied the corporeal presence in the bread and wine, forbade the use of vestments and ordered the replacement of the altar by a communion table to be placed east to west in the church rather than north to south, like a traditional altar. Swiss Reformed influence could also be seen in the official outbreaks of iconoclasm (the attack on religious images as idolatrous).

During the Edwardian Reformation there were undoubtedly many sincere conversions to Protestantism, but the evidence (unsatisfactory though it is) suggests that a majority of the population remained Catholic or conservative in their beliefs during the six years of the king's reign. As a result, from 1553 onwards Mary I had little difficulty in restoring many Catholic devotional practices in most parts of England, although it was proved impossible for her to extirpate Protestantism from the realm (Duffy 1992).

Mary's heresy laws forced committed Protestants into semiconformity, exile abroad or secret membership of underground congregations; in addition, several hundred Protestants became martyrs, burnt at the stake for their beliefs. These experiences of the brief English Counter-Reformation left their mark on the Protestants who survived and influenced the nature of the Elizabethan Church. Seventeen of Elizabeth's first generation of bishops and a significant number of her councillors, officials, clergy and academics had been exiles under Mary, and most of them found refuge in the Swiss Reformed centres of Europe, where they built up personal contacts with theologians like Heinrich Bullinger and Peter Martyr. There, they saw for themselves churches which had been torn from their papal past and had thoroughly reformed their theology, liturgy and discipline. Faced with these more advanced ideas, the exiles based in Frankfurt quarrelled among themselves about the form of worship and church government they should follow. One group, under the leadership of Richard Cox, was determined to keep to the Second Edwardian Prayer Book and 'do as they had done in England', but others, led by John Knox, preferred to follow the Calvinist model of reform. When they returned to England, all the exiles brought back with them the common ideal of uprooting popery from the Protestant Church and spiritually revitalizing the English people, but divisions remained between those who were content with a return to the 1552 Prayer Book and those who hoped for a more thorough reformation.

The smaller and less influential group of Protestants who remained in England but stayed away from their parish churches under Mary were no less affected by their experiences. Many of them had attended covert independent congregations and some had even devised their own forms of Protestant worship, under lay leadership. As a result, they had developed a radical and uncompromising approach to their religion which was to create problems for the ecclesiastical authorities under Elizabeth.

The Marian burnings too had an influence on religious attitudes in Elizabeth's reign. While their unpopularity under Mary has perhaps been exaggerated, there can be little doubt that, through the vivid accounts in John Foxe's *Acts and Monuments* or *Book of Martyrs*, published in 1563, the martyrdom of bishops, like Cranmer, and of ordinary men and women helped create strong anti-Catholic sentiment in Elizabethan England. In addition, Foxe's book helped form an English Protestant identity. Originally, Protestantism had been suspect as a foreign import, but the *Book of Martyrs* told the story of English heretics being burnt by a half-Spanish queen, through the influence of her Spanish husband and on behalf of a foreign pope. Foxe also used the sufferings of the martyrs 'under the great persecution and horrible troubles' of the Roman Catholic Church to vindicate the English Church as a true church in the eyes of God and men. In his narrative, English Protestants were re-enacting the story of the Old Testament, and like the children of Israel they came through their time of trial to ultimate triumph. For Foxe and his readers, therefore, the English Protestants were God's chosen people or 'elect nation' (Collinson 1988).

When Elizabeth came to the throne in November 1558, therefore, the religious situation was very difficult and complex. The country was not only divided between Catholics and Protestants, but also the Protestants themselves had different views about the nature and character of a reformed church as a result of the varied experiences of Mary's reign. Any decision made by the new regime on the religious future of the country would bring its own problems.

2

Elizabeth's religious views

Few historians today would agree with A. F. Pollard, in his history of England published in 1919, that Elizabeth 'was sceptical or indifferent in religion'; on the contrary most now accept that throughout her adult life she was a committed and conventionally pious Protestant. As an impressionable adolescent, she had been educated by the humanists, William Grindal and Roger Ascham, and immersed in the atmosphere of the evangelical households of Sir Anthony Denny and Queen Katherine Parr, Henry VIII's last wife. During the latter years of her father's reign, she had spent months in translating three pious works of an Erasmian or mildly Protestant nature into different languages: a French version of Erasmus's *Dialogus Fidei*, an English copy of Marguerite de Valois's *Mirror or Glass of the Sinful Soul*, and a version in French, Italian and Latin of her stepmother's composition, *Prayers or Meditations*. In the reign of her half-brother, she was noted for her 'godly zeal', an image that she was keen to cultivate. Throughout Mary's reign, she was a suspected heretic and continued to use the English Bible, even though she obeyed the law and attended the Catholic mass. Once queen, she not only regularly attended morning service in the royal chapel but in addition used private prayers, probably composed by herself, for daily worship (Haugaard 1981).

As soon as she was proclaimed queen, Elizabeth made clear to her subjects that she intended to introduce a Protestant Church Settlement. Her new streamlined Privy Council had a decidedly Protestant complexion, and her most important minister, Secretary William Cecil, had previously withdrawn from public life in 1553 rather than publicly endorse Catholicism. Before the end of 1558, Protestants who had been deprived of their livings or had gone into exile under Mary were invited to preach on public occasions, while Catholic preachers were harassed or arrested. For example, on the Sunday after her accession Elizabeth allowed Dr William Bill, a Protestant who had been ejected from Cambridge during the previous reign, to preach at St Paul's Cross, yet she arrested the bishop of Chichester for preaching a rejoinder the following Sunday. Even before her first parliament met, liturgical changes were introduced, first in her chapel and then in the realm. Proclamations of 27 and 28 December ordered the use of the Epistles, Gospels, Lord's Prayer, Creed and Litany in English until parliament decided on 'matters and ceremonies of religion'. On Christmas Day Elizabeth displayed her disbelief in the doctrine of transubstantiation when she walked out of her chapel service after the officiant, Bishop Oglethorpe, refused to obey her instructions not to elevate the host (the consecrated bread). At her coronation in January 1559, there was no elevation of the host, nor were the bread and wine consecrated by the priest. When parliament eventually met some three months after the accession, the Lord Keeper, acting as governmental spokesman, called upon the members to consider the 'well making of laws for the according and uniting of the people of this realm into a uniform order of religion', which was a clear indication that Elizabeth intended to introduce a Prayer Book and a uniformity bill (Jones 1982).

For these reasons, few historians today would accept the view expressed by Sir John Neale in 1953 that Elizabeth only wanted an interim Church Settlement in 1559, one which would return England to the religious situation on her father's death – Catholicism without the Pope – and that she only changed her mind as a result of pressure from Protestant MPs during the first session of the 1559 Parliament (Haigh 1984). But while there is now a general consensus that Elizabeth intended to go further than her father and impose the Protestant religion on her subjects, historians still disagree about the exact form of Protestantism she wanted. Some, like William P. Haugaard, argue that she would have preferred the re-introduction of the more conservative 1549 Prayer Book of Edward VI, had her lay and clerical advisers agreed to it (Haugaard 1970). On the other hand, Winthrop Hudson and Norman Jones are convinced that she planned the settlement which finally emerged, one based on the Second Edwardian Prayer Book of 1552 (Hudson 1980; Jones 1982). There is, however, no clear answer to this dispute, since so many records relating to the formulation of the 1559 Church Settlement have not survived and Elizabeth's own statements about her religious preferences were so ambiguous.

None the less, whichever Prayer Book Elizabeth would have preferred, it is certain that she was anxious to retain some Catholic ceremonial and traditions within her Church for both personal and political reasons. She personally disliked the idea of a married clergy, had a love of elaborate church music, and refused to accept that all images were idolatrous and proscribed in the Bible. At the same time, she was aware of the importance of persuading the Catholic powers, especially Spain, that her Church was little different in external appearance from theirs, in order to prevent a papal crusade against her and Spanish diplomatic support for Mary Stuart, the Catholic claimant to the English throne. She also needed to convince the Lutheran princes of Germany that she was a follower of their Augsburg Confession (the Lutheran statement of doctrine which had been drawn up in 1530) so that they would agree to a defensive alliance with England. Outward Catholic signs, such as the use of vestments, crosses and candlesticks, would serve to reassure both Lutherans and Catholics that England was an acceptable friend and had not entered the despised Calvinist camp. Consequently, Elizabeth tried to temper the Protestant enthusiasm of some of her clergy and insisted that the outward form of her Church – its liturgy, furniture and ministerial dress – should remain as traditional as possible. The Royal Injunctions of 1559 were part of this policy, but in addition she sanctioned the use of a Latin Prayer Book in the universities and in the colleges of Winchester and Eton in 1560. In 1560 and 1561 she issued proclamations which tried to limit damage to the furniture of the parish churches and cathedrals – funeral monuments, fonts, bells, steeples and porches. During 1559 and 1560 she had a tussle (which she finally won) with the archbishop of Canterbury and other divines over her determination to keep a silver cross or crucifix and two candlesticks 'standing altarwise' in the royal chapel (Haugaard 1970).

Thus, although the precise nature of Elizabeth's Protestantism is not known, from her actions it appears that she hardly moved on from the evangelical lessons of her youth and never came to embrace the more radical doctrines of the Swiss Reformed Church. As a result, she found herself in a kind of time-warp, once she had succeeded to the throne, and out of sympathy with the aspirations of her divines to reform the English Church more thoroughly and bring it into line with the model church of Geneva.

3

The Parliament of 1559

As shown in Chapter 2, Elizabeth's government intended to introduce a religious settlement in 1559 which would enforce a Protestant form of service through an Act of Uniformity. It also planned to introduce an Act of Supremacy which would legitimize this royal reformation of the Church. Opposition to the legislative programme, however, was mounted by Catholic activists, led by the bishops in the House of Lords, whose resistance was so vigorous that the supremacy and uniformity bills nearly foundered. They were eventually passed only because the queen effectively applied a mixture of compromise and coercion, by making some concessions to appease the consciences of the laity and by weakening episcopal solidarity through arrests and intimidation. As a result of the bishops' refusal to accept the supremacy even after it became law, Elizabeth had to rely on the Marian exiles and other zealous Protestants to fill vacant positions in the Church and enforce the new religious settlement. The new leadership of the English Church was therefore more committed to Protestant reform than Elizabeth would ideally have wished.

The parliamentary session of 1559 opened on 25 January, and on 9 February the House of Commons heard the first reading of a supremacy bill. It was followed on 15 and 16 February by the reading of one or two bills designed to introduce Protestant forms of worship, which were almost certainly governmental measures and not the private members' bills suggested by Professor Neale (Neale 1953). The story of these bills' passage through the Commons has been described as 'one of the great unsolved mysteries of sixteenth-century parliamentary history' since very little documentation has survived (Loach 1991). The records simply show that at the committee stage the bills were fused together, and a new composite bill was passed in the Commons on 23 February after a 'stormy debate' (Jones 1982).

Few historians now believe that the proceedings in the Commons were influenced by a powerful party of zealous Protestants who had returned from exile. The House, in fact, contained far fewer active and vocal Protestants than was once assumed; only some twenty or twenty-five members can be identified as radical Protestants, eight of whom had been exiled for religious reasons in the previous reign, while another twenty or so can be reckoned as committed Catholics. The religion of the vast majority cannot be detected, but it is likely that most were prepared to vote in support of whatever governmental legislation was proposed. The main concern of some of these MPs was to keep their title to the church lands purchased under Henry VIII and his son and to regain the lands which they had lost when Mary restored various manors taken from episcopal sees by Edward VI and passed on by him to the laity. This anxiety about church lands smoothed the way to their acceptance of the royal supremacy since the MPs knew that they could never feel secure in their ownership of confiscated ecclesiastical property while the Pope kept his jurisdiction over England. The Commons spent three weeks on private bills concerning the Marian restorations, during which time the new composite bill was debated in the House of Lords.

In the House of Lords, the opponents of religious change were numerous and influential. Of the seventy-seven peers who had the right to speak, some twenty-four lay lords preferred to see the retention of the mass, while all the seventeen spiritual peers were opposed to the supremacy as well. In practice, however, attendance in the House never exceeded forty-five peers, of whom eighteen opposed changes in doctrine. In the bill's committee stage, the Catholics dominated the proceedings and the uniformity clauses were dropped, though agreement was reached that communion in both kinds should be allowed (both the wine and the bread should be offered to the laity and not just the bread as happened in the Catholic Church). As far as the supremacy was concerned, the queen was told that she could use the title of 'Supreme Head' if she so chose, but the Lords would not grant it to her. The emasculated bill then came back to the Commons on 18 March and was reluctantly passed on 22 March. Two days later the queen prorogued the Parliament for its Easter recess.

Elizabeth and Cecil were surprised by the Lords' attack on their legislation, since in the past most of the bishops and lay lords had accepted royal policy on religion. For a while they considered dissolving parliament and leaving well alone, but, as the queen's legal position might then become untenable and the unstable religious situation might create political unrest, they decided to hold a second session and try again to obtain parliamentary sanction of the royal supremacy and Protestant settlement. Their first step was to discredit and intimidate the bishops by holding a public disputation of divines at Westminster Abbey which was rigged against the Catholics. Immediately after the debate, the bishops of Lincoln and Winchester were sent to the Tower charged with disobedience.

The second session of parliament met on 3 April, and a week later a new supremacy bill was read in the Commons. To make it more palatable to the Catholics who would recognize no other than the Pope as head of the Church, the queen's title in the bill was changed from 'Supreme Head' to 'Supreme Governor'. In addition, the bill contained clauses which repealed the Marian heresy laws and allowed communion in both kinds, perhaps as an insurance policy in case the conscience of the Catholics allowed them to pass this measure but baulked at the separate uniformity bill. The supremacy bill passed the Commons quite easily and, though again meeting resistance in the Lords, eventually passed there too on 26 April, despite the opposition of all the spiritual lords and one lay lord, Lord Montague.

On 18 April a uniformity bill was introduced in the Commons. When it reached the Lords, it also met opposition; indeed it came very close to defeat on the final vote when nine laymen joined the bishops in voting against it, making eighteen votes against and twenty-one in its favour. Had the two bishops not been in the Tower and one abbot inexplicably absent, the Catholic opposition would have been successful. Soon after the legislation was passed on 28 April, all the Marian bishops save the octogenarian Anthony Kitchin of Llandaff refused to take the statutory Oath of Supremacy and were deprived, their vacant sees being filled by zealous Protestants.

The second session of the 1559 Parliament passed one further bill of significance in the history of the Elizabethan Church: the Act of Exchange. By this measure the queen was empowered to take the temporal property (manors or castles) of a vacant episcopal see and in exchange would grant to the affected bishopric impropriated spiritualities (tithes and advowsons taken over by the Crown when the monasteries were dissolved) which were of the same yearly value as the temporal property taken. This Act followed bills which confiscated the lands of the few Marian monasteries and chantries and which restored first fruits and tenths to the monarch. It therefore extended the principle beloved by the Tudors that ecclesiastical property could be taken over by the Crown.

4

The Elizabethan Church Settlement

The legal basis of the English Church was laid down not only in the 1559 Acts of Supremacy and Uniformity but also in the Royal Injunctions of 1559 and the Thirty-Nine Articles of Religion, which were passed in the convocation of 1563 but did not become part of statutory law until 1571.

The Act of Supremacy gave Elizabeth the new title of Supreme Governor of the Church of England. Although designed to placate the Catholics, the change also pleased some Protestants who believed that the headship of the Church 'is due to Christ alone, and cannot belong to any human being soever', and were particularly uneasy at the prospect of a woman assuming a quasi-priestly role in the Church (Cross 1969). The new title, however, made no difference in practice to the extent of royal authority over the Church, as Elizabeth exercised the same rights over religion as had her father, and was determined to keep religion firmly under the control of the Crown. Her attitude was symbolized by the placing of the royal arms within the parish churches in the place where the rood (the crucifix flanked by carved images of the Virgin Mary and St John) had once stood as an object of communal worship.

The Act of Uniformity imposed compulsory attendance at church on Sundays and Holy Days and sanctioned a new Prayer Book, which contained a few changes from its 1552 predecessor. The most important modifications lay in the communion service

14

and the Ornaments Rubric and were conservative in nature. In the communion service, the Elizabethan minister was required to insert two additional sentences from the 1549 Prayer Book at the point of offering the bread and wine to the communicant. When giving the bread, he would utter the formula of 1549, 'The Body of our Lord Jesus Christ, which was given for thee, preserve thy body and soul unto everlasting life', just before saying the words from the 1552 Book, 'take and eat this in remembrance that Christ died for thee, and feed on him in thy heart by faith with thanksgiving' (Regan 1988). The effect of joining together the two formulae was doctrinally significant, as it allowed the possibility of belief that Christ's body and blood were really present in the bread and wine, so important to both Catholics and Lutherans, while at the same time asserting the memorial aspect of the service, which conformed to the theology of the Swiss Reformed Church. At the same time, the 1559 rubric (directions for the conduct of the service) for the administration of communion omitted the so-called 'Black Rubric' in the 1552 Prayer Book, which had contained an explicit denial of the corporeal presence. This compromise was a liturgical masterstroke as it allowed all types of Protestants to participate in the communion service with a clear conscience (MacCulloch 1990).

The Ornaments Rubric adopted in 1559 was less successful in satisfying all Protestant opinion. The rubric, inserted before Morning and Evening Prayer, ordered that the ornaments for the churches and their ministers should be those in use 'by authority of parliament' in the second year of Edward VI's reign. Hence, churches should keep their crosses, candlesticks and other furnishings, and ministers were expected to don the alb and cope (Catholic vestments traditionally worn at mass) at communion, and to wear a surplice (a loose white linen overgarment) at all other services. The returning Marian exiles particularly disliked these prescriptions but hoped that in the short term Elizabeth would not enforce the rubric and that in the longer term she would revoke it, since the Act of Uniformity reserved to the queen the right to change the ornaments and other rites whenever such alterations were necessary. In this belief, however, they were mistaken, and their misunderstanding created tensions between Elizabeth and her Protestant clergy early in the reign.

Some of the Royal Injunctions which were issued in July 1559 extended the conservative modifications to the new Prayer Book and proved to be a great disappointment to the Marian exiles who wanted to see all traces of popery removed from the English Church. Injunction Thirty not only reinforced the Ornaments Rubric on clerical dress, but also ordered the clergy to don distinctive clothes for everyday wear. Other injunctions encouraged the use of church music in the Sunday service, even though the Calvinists at Geneva had banned elaborate music and only permitted the unaccompanied singing of metrical psalms. The queen also ordered or allowed the continuation of several practices which had been condemned as superstitious by the Swiss Reformed Church. Thus, congregations were told to uncover and bow their heads at the name of Jesus, unleavened bread (bread which had not risen and looked like wafers) could be used at communion instead of ordinary bread, and images were excluded from the list of 'things tending to idolatry and superstition' which needed to be defaced or destroyed. As far as images were concerned, Elizabeth clearly wanted to avoid the wholesale iconoclasm of her brother's reign (Aston 1988).

Relatively few of the Royal Injunctions pushed England further down the road of reformation, but there were some which focused on improving the education of both the clergy and laity and others which required monthly sermons to be heard in parishes instead of the quarterly sermons of Edward VI's reign (Cross 1969). The injunctions also provided practical commandments for the observance of holy days, enjoining that they should be spent hearing the word of God or doing godly work such as visiting the poor and sick (Parker 1987). A number of the injunctions permitted Protestant practices legalized under Edward, which Elizabeth did not like but agreed to rather grudgingly. Thus, she allowed clerical marriage, but prospective wives had to be examined and approved by the diocesan bishop and two JPs, 'because there hath grown offence, and some slander to the church by lack of discreet and sober behaviour in many ministers of the church, both in choosing of their wives, and undiscreet living with them' (Cross 1969).

The injunctions formed the basis for a royal visitation of the whole country which began on 19 July 1559. The royal commissioners were dominated by returned Marian exiles who were totally committed to a radical reform of religion and destruction of all vestiges of popery. Consequently, they embarked on a wholesale destruction of Catholic externals, whether images, altars or vestments, until the queen intervened by issuing proclamations to protect ancient monuments, fonts and altars (Duffy 1992).

Partly as a result of the ambiguities in the 1559 Settlement, the liturgy of the Elizabethan Church allowed for a great deal of local variation. Some parish churches as well as most of the cathedrals emphasized the ceremonial aspects of the 1559 Prayer Book. In these churches, the service would be sung with 'modest and distinct song'; an elaborate hymn sometimes accompanied by an organ would end morning or evening prayer; and to take communion the congregation would walk from the nave through to the chancel, where they would kneel to receive a wafer and sip of wine from a chalice offered by a minister in full vestments. At the same time, in other parishes of England the liturgy of the Elizabethan Church came to be performed in the austere manner favoured by the Reformed Church. In these churches, ministers wore no vestments, portable tables were brought down to the nave of the church for the communion service, the wine was drunk from a cup and, like the bread, was received sitting or standing, and there was no music at all except for organ voluntaries and the congregational singing of the psalms in metre. Almost everywhere, however, even in the cathedrals, the sermon, not communion, was at the centre of the Sunday service, as communion became celebrated only monthly and lengthy sermons were delivered more than once a week.

The 1559 Settlement established by the queen in parliament contained no statement of faith. Since Elizabeth believed that the responsibility for theology lay with the clergy and not parliament, a definition of doctrine had to await the appointment of a new Protestant bench of bishops. Elizabeth was probably content to keep silent on the issue of doctrine in 1559, as she wanted to avoid further antagonizing Catholics at home and abroad, as well as taking sides in the theological disputes which were dividing Protestant Europe. Her new Protestant episcopate, however, was very keen to get down to the task of establishing the doctrine of the English Church, since it believed that a statement of faith was essential to the work of teaching the Gospels. Therefore at the very first opportunity offered to them, the bishops drew up the Thirty-Nine Articles of Faith (Horie 1991).

Although most of the bishops had been exiles in the Swiss Reformed centres of Europe during Mary's reign, they were anxious to frame a statement which would be acceptable to both the Lutheran and Swiss Reformed Churches on the Continent so that there could be a united front against the Catholics, who had been re-defining their own doctrines at the Council of Trent. As a result the bishops emphasized, wherever possible, common ground between the two main Protestant confessions. About one third of the Articles expressed ecumenical Christian beliefs, several upheld doctrines shared by both Lutherans and Calvinists, and six specifically refuted the teachings alleged to be held by the Anabaptists (radical Protestant sects) (Haugaard 1970). On the issues dividing the Lutheran and Swiss Reformed Churches, the bishops tried to reach a compromise, which would satisfy both. On the contentious issue of the Eucharist, Article Twenty-Eight affirmed that 'the Body of Christ is given, taken and eaten in the Supper only after an heavenly and spiritual manner. And the mean whereby the Body of Christ is received and eaten in the Supper is Faith.' Although this form of words denied that Christ was physically present in the bread and wine, a doctrine which was so important to the Lutherans, it did imply that communion was more than just a memorial of the sacrifice of Christ, as the Zwinglians believed. The bishops who wrote the Article also tried to avoid offending the Lutherans by omitting any denial of the 'ubiquity' of Christ, the notion devised by some of Luther's heirs that Christ could be present everywhere in creation. Article Twenty-Nine was, however, more abhorrent to the Lutherans, as it challenged their belief that grace was offered to all Christians in its statement that the 'Wicked and such as be void of a lively faith' are not 'partakers of Christ' at the Lord's Supper 'but rather to their condemnation, do eat and drink the sign or Sacrament of so great a thing'. It was for this reason that Elizabeth, possibly on the advice of Cecil who was seeking an alliance with the German Protestant princes, omitted this clause from all printed editions of the articles until 1571. On predestination, Article Seventeen was deliberately ambiguous in order to be acceptable to both Lutherans and the Swiss Reformed Churches. Thus, it asserted election and predestination in its statement, 'Predestination to Life is the everlasting purpose of God, whereby (before the foundations of the world were laid) he hath constantly decreed by his counsel, secret to us, to deliver from curse and damnation those whom he hath chosen in Christ out of mankind'; and it echoed the optimism of Martin Bucer that belief in predestination strengthened one's faith and was 'full of sweet, pleasant and unspeakable comfort to godly persons'. At the same time, however, it omitted reference to all Calvinist doctrines about predestination and avoided stating unequivocally that the reprobate faced eternal damnation (Haugaard 1970; Horie 1991).

In its liturgy and theology, therefore, the early Elizabethan Church was something of a hybrid, containing features that were Lutheran, Zwinglian and Calvinist. Some historians think that little or no change took place during the whole reign and that Calvinism remained a minority view within the Elizabethan Church. The majority of scholars, however, argue convincingly that the theology of the Church moved in a more Zwinglian and Calvinist direction as the reign progressed (Lake 1987). Elizabeth's first generation of bishops retained their commitment to Reformed theology and kept up their close links with the Swiss Reformers, Peter Martyr, Heinrich Bullinger, Rudolph Gualter and Theodore Beza, Calvin's successor at Geneva. Through their influence, many of the official publications of the English Church, the sermons and theological treatises came increasingly to reflect the outlook and doctrines of the Swiss Reformed Churches, especially on the doctrine of double predestination. The catechism written by Anthony Nowell, which became the authorized textbook for children after 1571, not only assumed belief in predestination but also borrowed directly from Calvin's own catechism; 28 per cent of Nowell's lines bear a close resemblance to the words of Calvin, including his section on the Eucharist. The Geneva Bible, which was first published in 1560, contained Calvinist comments on the scriptures in its marginalia, and it was so widely purchased after 1570 that a further edition appeared in 1578 and another sixteen editions were published between 1578 and 1583. Its rival, the Bishop's Bible of 1568, also included marginalia which promoted the Calvinist line on predestination. By 1600 there had been some ninety editions of Calvin's works published in English.

Calvinist doctrines were soon absorbed by English preachers and theologians. Between 1570 and the end of the reign, only one of the sermons preached at St Paul's Cross expressed anti-

Calvinist views, and its author (Samuel Harsnett) was reprimanded by the authorities as a result. Towards the end of the reign Calvinist teaching on predestination dominated the University of Oxford and was strong in Cambridge, although it never secured the same intellectual hold there. By the 1590s all the leading bishops were imbued with the Calvinist theology of predestination, including John Whitgift, archbishop of Canterbury, and Matthew Hutton, who was archbishop of York from 1595. Even Richard Bancroft, known as the scourge of the Puritans in James's reign, personally licensed in 1598 the publication of a Calvinist treatise which denied that Christ had died for all mankind and asserted the doctrine of unconditional predestination.

In 1595 several divines, including Archbishop John Whitgift and Richard Fletcher, bishop of London, approved, with some amendments, a statement on the doctrine of predestination drawn up by a group of Cambridge theology dons. Known as the Lambeth Articles, it asserted belief in double predestination and the eternal decree: that 'God from eternity predestined certain men to life and condemned others to death' and that 'the number of the predestined is prescribed and certain and it cannot be increased or diminished'. The Articles also stated the Calvinist belief in 'assurance': that faith 'is not extinguished, does not leave or disappear in the elect either finally or totally', and that a man with justifying faith is 'certain' of 'his eternal salvation through Christ'. The queen, however, refused to give legal status to the Articles, not only because she disliked them but also because she disapproved of the unilateral action of her archbishop in approving them, especially as he had tried to keep their existence a secret from her (Cross 1969). As a result of their suppression, Calvinist orthodoxy, though dominant in the Church, never became part of its official confession.

While the Elizabethan Church came to be Calvinist in its mainstream theology after 1570, its discipline moved only haphazardly and partially away from its Catholic past. Archbishop Parker appeared to favour the establishment of a Protestant code of ecclesiastical law based on Thomas Cranmer's 1553 *Reformatio Legum Ecclesiasticarum* (Reform of Ecclesiastical Law), which among its other canons (ecclesiastical laws) made provision for a system of parochial and diocesan discipline. The clergy at the 1563 Convocation discussed the formulation of ecclesiastical laws and discipline, but no reform emerged, for reasons which are obscure. In 1571, Cranmer's son-in-law, Thomas Norton, introduced the *Reform* into the House of Commons as a bill; but although this probably had the support of the bishops and some privy councillors, it was lost in committee. Parker then drew up his own canons of discipline, which the bishops accepted at the 1571 Convocation. If legally enforced, Parker's code would have established a system of discipline in England akin to that seen in Reformed cities on the Continent, with church-wardens acting as elders responsible for overseeing the moral behaviour of the ministers and laity. Parker's code, however, had an uncertain legal authority, since it was ratified neither by parliament nor by the queen herself in writing. Elizabeth argued that the canons had the force of law, as an act of convocation authorized by her supremacy, but in reality, without the confirmation of parliament or the express ratification of the queen, the code was unenforceable, or so the bishops believed. Consequently, it was only applied in a piecemeal fashion in areas which were keen to introduce a Reformed system of discipline (Spalding 1992).

The ecclesiastical government of the Elizabethan Church was even more distant from the model of Geneva. Not only did the English Church retain its bishops, archdeacons, cathedrals and dioceses; it found no official place for Calvin's four-fold ministry of pastors, elders, doctors, and deacons elected by individual congregations and the network of representative assemblies – local classes, provincial and national synods – which linked the individual churches together. It was far closer to the Lutheran model of an Erastian Church, or even to the Catholic Church, though without the Pope and cardinals.

Because of the hybrid nature of the Elizabethan Church, the Settlement of 1559 and 1563 has often been described as a *via media*, a middle way between Rome and Geneva. Such a label, however, is misleading, since it implies that a *via media* was the well-thought-out principle upon which the Church was founded. In reality, the nature of the Church was greatly influenced by pragmatic political considerations, and its shape was formed as a result of serious tensions between the queen and her divines, which were never completely settled.

Similarly, it is misleading to describe the official position of the Elizabethan Church as 'Anglican' and to call the official religion of the country 'Anglicanism'. The very name 'Anglicanism' emphasizes the uniquely English character of the Elizabethan Church and implies that it was nationalistic and self-consciously different from Protestant Churches on the Continent. Using the word 'Anglicanism' reinforces the idea that the English Church followed a unique 'middle way' in the history of Protestantism: Protestant but not Calvinist in theology; ceremony-centred but not popish; reformed yet episcopalian.

As already seen, however, the Elizabethan Church was not at all cut off from the European Reformation. Its most committed and articulate members were conscious of a solidarity with the Reformed Churches on the Continent; hence, its leading clergy regularly communicated with Bullinger, Beza and the rest, while laity and ministers alike concerned themselves with the fate of their co-religionists abroad. During 1582 and 1583, for example, some £6000 was raised by public collection for the city of Geneva, then under attack by the duke of Savoy. Furthermore, the ethos of the Elizabethan Church was Reformed; its leadership was wedded to the Calvinist approach to predestination, sabbatarianism (strict observance of the Lord's Day) and the importance of preaching, and there was no serious debate on these issues until the 1590s. The iconophobia (hatred of images) of mainstream Protestants had not only revolutionized the interiors of churches but percolated downwards to disturb popular culture; during the Elizabethan period pictures disappeared from religious books and began to be rare as household possessions (Collinson 1988).

For these reasons, the word 'Anglicanism' is now being expunged from the vocabulary of Elizabethan historians and students; it was certainly not used at the time and only gained recognition in the nineteenth century, when Anglo-Catholic churchmen wanted to claim that their vision of the Church was not novel but the natural heir of an Anglican tradition going back to the Elizabethan Church Settlement (MacCulloch 1991). Today too the most conservative members of the Church of England favour the word 'Anglican', and trace their views back to the Elizabethan Reformation, even though their doctrines on the priesthood and the Eucharist have little in common with those laid down in the 1559 Settlement.

5

The Puritans

Definitions

Puritanism has traditionally been defined in relation to Anglicanism, since historians viewed it as the radical Protestant alternative to the Anglican Church and the ideology of a small but assertive opposition group who wanted to align the Church of England with the Reformed Church on the Continent. Puritans were, therefore, usually described as Calvinists or as reformers who wanted to purge the Anglican Church of its Catholic features.

The redefinition of mainstream Protestantism and rejection of the name 'Anglicanism' clearly posed a problem for historians used to treating Puritans in this way. It now became clear that there was no profound theological cleavage within the Elizabethan Church but that on the contrary there was in general a 'Calvinist consensus' (Lake 1987). With this revision, a new definition of Puritanism was clearly required but it was not easy to find. Puritans were not an easily identified group within the Church who held distinct opinions about doctrine, liturgy and discipline; nor were they merely a reforming group who saw the 1559 Settlement as temporary and endeavoured to obtain further instalments of reform, for this could equally well be said of the early Elizabethan bishops. Frustrated by the difficulties of finding a clear definition which could be used to distinguish

23

Puritans from mainstream Protestants who were also Reformed in their outlook and reformers in their intentions, some historians have given up the struggle for precision and have discarded the word 'Puritan' along with 'Anglican'. Others, such as Paul Christianson, have responded to the problem by defining 'Puritan' more narrowly, and limiting it to Presbyterians and hardened nonconformists who would not obey the orders of the bishops yet did not separate themselves from the Church of England and accepted the royal supremacy, albeit with some reservations (Christianson 1980).

Both these approaches, however, dissatisfied Patrick Collinson and Peter Lake, the two foremost authorities on Elizabethan Puritanism. As Professor Collinson has pointed out, unlike 'Anglican', the term 'Puritan' is not anachronistic but on the contrary was a term of abuse used by contemporaries and as such had a meaning at the time, however imprecisely the word was employed. Furthermore, explains Collinson, some of the contemporary understanding of the word would be lost if historians confined its usage to a clear category of ministers who were noted for their nonconformity or Presbyterianism, since all kinds of people, laity as well as clergy, were stigmatized as 'Puritans' in the late Elizabethan period. Dr Lake agrees and also prefers historians to use a broader if less precise definition of 'Puritan' than that suggested by Christianson (Lake 1988).

For both Collinson and Lake, Puritans were Protestants, both lay and clerical, whose religious enthusiasm and zeal marked them off from their more lukewarm contemporaries. They were a self-conscious group who were totally committed to purging the Established Church of its popish 'superstitions' and bringing a biblical morality to English society. They called themselves the 'godly', and this title is sometimes used by historians interchangeably with Puritan. As with every group, the Puritans ranged from the moderate to the radical: the radical element was particularly obstreperous in its refusal to compromise its principles by conforming to practices within the Church that it considered ungodly, and often drifted into Presbyterianism; the moderates, on the other hand, did not refuse to conform when pressed hard by the ecclesiastical authorities, but did so reluctantly and under protest for fear that their refusal to conform would result in their loss of a living or preaching licence and thus jeopardize the preaching ministry.

The importance in forming this definition of Puritan, however, is not that a label now exists to describe this or that individual; there is little mileage in trying to decide whether men like Bishop Edmund Grindal or the earl of Leicester were Puritans or merely patrons of Puritans. Its importance lies elsewhere; as Professor Collinson has explained, the incidence of the term in contemporary writings indicates to historians the existence of theological, moral and social tensions in Elizabethan England, and a study of its use throws light on those tensions (Christianson 1980). Collinson's own earliest study of the Elizabethan Puritan movement focused on the political conflicts which emerged with the development of nonconformity and Presbyterianism, but thereafter he has been concerned to investigate the tensions in society arising from the distinct lifestyle of the godly (Collinson 1967 and 1982). Dr Lake has tended to concentrate on analysing the theological divides within the Calvinist consensus (Lake 1988).

The term 'Puritan' was first coined during the so-called Vestiarian Controversy of the mid-1560s to describe the zealots who resisted conforming to the conservative rubrics laid down in the 1559 Prayer Book; and throughout the Elizabethan period those ministers who refused to conform to all the rituals and rubrics laid down in the Prayer Book were called Puritans or precisionists by their enemies. In the 1570s, a small group of Presbyterians became the radical wing of the Puritan movement, rather in the same way that Socialists are at the extreme end of the Labour Party today. Finally, by the end of the reign when the Presbyterian movement had been effectively destroyed, the term 'Puritan' was used more generally to slur 'the hotter sort of Protestants' who followed a godly life-style which separated them from their neighbours.

All these kinds of Puritans shared a common outlook, and one that marked them off from Protestants who were ready to use 'Puritan' as a term of abuse. Dr Lake's study of the arguments forwarded in the Admonition Controversy of the 1570s (see pp. 34–6) has done much to clarify the differences between Puritans like the first Elizabethan Presbyterian, Thomas Cartwright, and their opponents, like John Whitgift. As both Cartwright and Whitgift were committed Calvinists, they did of course share a common Protestant world-view. They both believed in double predestination; they took the words of the scriptures literally and used them as the ultimate authority in any debate; and they had an intense hatred of both popery and Anabaptism.

Within this basic Protestant consensus, however, Cartwright and Whitgift disagreed fundamentally on several important theological issues. The first concerned adiaphora. 'Adiaphora' were religious beliefs and practices which were neither commanded nor condemned in the scriptures and could therefore be considered relatively trivial or 'matters indifferent'. Whitgift argued that all things indifferent, including the form of ecclesiastical government, could be determined by the human authority of the royal supremacy since they were not ordained by God. In other words, if the queen chose to order the wearing of vestments and to use bishops to run her Church, this was entirely permissible as the scriptures laid down no clear directions on these matters. Cartwright, on the other hand, argued that even adiaphora had to be regulated according to criteria which were laid down in the scriptures. For this reason, he urged the abolition of vestments, kneeling at communion, the ring in marriage and other 'popish' ceremonies, as he believed that they contravened the biblical injunctions to edify and to avoid offending the godly.

The second difference between the two men related to their approach to predestination. Both were 'credal predestinarians' in that they accepted Calvinist teaching on predestination. Cartwright, however, can also be called an 'experimental predestinarian', as he was anxious to lead his life in accordance with a strict and literal interpretation of predestination. He wanted to separate the reprobate from the elect in this world and not wait for God to do it in the next. The reprobate, he believed, should be excluded from the Church; and so sinners and papists should be cut off from the elect by excommunication, and their children left unbaptized. Whitgift, however, opposed the separation of the visible and invisible Churches (the invisible Church is the community of the elect), as it would lead to a dangerous sectarianism which would threaten the existence of a national Church. Arguing that the visible Church was the 'net of the Lord' which caught many fish, he believed that baptism should be open to all and anyone who was not a notorious sinner should be allowed communion.

Their different approaches to predestination were reinforced by different attitudes to edification. Cartwright believed that the central role of the Church was to edify, by which he meant that its primary task was to build up the spiritual life of its members and help them achieve the godliness that was the hallmark of the elect. In order to do this effectively, the Church had to be a pure and perfect institution, unpolluted by papistry and unsullied by sinners. As a result, the ungodly, who for him were roughly the same people as the reprobate, had to be cast out, the liturgy and government of the Church had to conform to God's injunctions, and the Word had to be preached so that all the elect could hear it. By contrast, Whitgift had little sense of edification, and for him the Church's main public function was to teach Christ's message rather than to engender an active spirituality among the elect. He was also less alarmed by the Church's inadequacies. Since the elect could not fall from grace, he was confident that salvation was not affected by inadequate preaching nor by imperfections in the Church and was satisfied that the presence of the profane in the visible Church in no way compromised the spiritual safety of the godly.

Finally, it should be noted that Cartwright had a greater fear of the power of evil and the forces of Anti-Christ than had Whitgift. As Calvinists, both men were profoundly pessimistic about human nature, but Cartwright believed that the forces of Anti-Christ were so insidious, pervasive and supernaturally strong that no opening could be allowed for them to enter. This too explains his extreme anxiety that all popery should be uprooted, all sinners cut off, and that the Church should follow the scriptures in the smallest detail and not introduce any unscriptural forms of worship, since all human inventions were liable to error, superstition and the influence of Anti-Christ. Whitgift was far less paranoid about the power of Anti-Christ. He had confidence that the Church was capable of identifying and controlling false doctrine, popery and sin through its use of order and discipline. Consequently, he had little fear that corruptions in the Church were chinks in its armour which would be exploited by the forces of Anti-Christ if not immediately eliminated. On the contrary, he believed that imperfections in the Church were inevitable as all human institutions were subject to change and decay.

Even though moderate Puritans did not accept Cartwright's Presbyterianism, they did share his approach to adiaphora, predestinarianism and edification. Like Cartwright they were 'experimental' predestinarians, who wanted to be 'assured' of their own elect status by experiencing God personally and following godly behaviour in their everyday lives. As a consequence, they tended to be more anti-papal, more fundamentalist in their treatment of the scriptures and more concerned with edification than their Protestant neighbours. Their religious life was more intense and was not limited to the parish church but extended to private devotions in the household and to various voluntary forms of public worship. At home, both individually and in family groups, Puritans studied the Bible, learnt the Calvinist catechism, read devotional manuals, composed their own spontaneous prayers, sang psalms, meditated and wrote diaries which recorded their spiritual progress and agonizings. On Sundays they not only attended their parish church in the morning, but spent the afternoon or evening in private meetings with like-minded neighbours repeating and learning the lessons of the sermons and reading together the Bible or Foxe's *Book of Martyrs*. Their thirst for bible-reading and sermons was unquenchable; on weekdays they listened to lectures or extracts from the scriptures in local churches, and on market-days they travelled in groups to nearby towns for the same purpose, singing psalms on the way. Periodically, in response to a particular trial or affliction, a whole day would be set aside for a public fast, which consisted of a course of sermons interrupted by prayers and psalm-singing, and which ended with the sharing of a communal meal and the collection of funds for a particular cause (Collinson 1982).

For reasons of edification, Puritans urged that the moral commandments of the Old Testament should be upheld by the laws of the realm. While not all would have agreed with Cartwright that Sabbath-breakers should face the death-penalty, they did expect transgressors to be publicly humiliated, fined for a first offence and excommunicated if they persisted in their sin. Like Cartwright, they wanted unrepentant fornicators, adulterers, drunkards and blasphemers to be thrown out of the visible Church, and so they criticized the ecclesiastical courts for meting out only 'toyish censures' for serious sin. The zeal of the Puritans led them not merely to complain, but to take action. In order to prevent temptation and a drift towards ungodliness, many Puritan magistrates tried to close the local alehouses, to shut down the theatres and to prohibit dances on the village green. To discipline offenders, Puritan ministers and lay people sometimes set up their own form of consistory court which existed alongside the official ecclesiastical courts. Some historians have suggested that it was not only Puritans who wanted a reformation of manners in the late sixteenth century, and have asserted that socio-economic factors rather than religious ideology lay behind the drives to regulate social and moral behaviour (Spufford 1974). Local studies of certain towns and villages, such as Terling in Essex, however, have produced strong evidence that Puritanism did influence the intensity of the attempts to suppress immorality. In the words of Ian Archer, a historian of Elizabethan London: 'The difference that religion makes . . . lies in the intensity of the campaign, rather than its presence or absence (Archer 1991).' One symptom of that intensity was the readiness of Puritans to punish people higher up the social scale, such as when the Puritan governors of Bridewell Hospital disciplined not only London prostitutes but their better-off male clients.

During the second half of the Elizabethan period, this kind of ethical and spiritual Puritanism thrived in many areas of England and remained part of mainstream Protestantism. In the words of Professor Collinson: 'puritans composed within the Church and nation a religious sub-culture of committed rather than merely formal and conventional Protestantism which if not separated, was distinct and, in the language of the age, "singular"' (Collinson 1982). At the same time, however, it must be emphasized that Puritans did not hold a distinctive social philosophy about usury, social control, philanthropy and a capitalist economy, as Christopher Hill once argued, or share a distinctive set of values about issues like marriage, work and sex, as Richard Greaves has postulated (Greaves 1981). Not only was there no divide between Puritans and other Protestants in their views on social questions, but also many late sixteenth-century social attitudes developed not from Calvinist teachings, as Hill and Greaves both assumed, but rather sprang from Christian humanist thinking and hence were shared by all kinds of Christians, including Roman Catholics abroad (Todd 1987).

To sum up, Puritans were not members of a separatist sect standing outside the Church of England, nor were they members of an opposition group in the House of Commons. They cannot be distinguished from conformist Protestants by their belief in a predestinarian theology, or in a Presbyterian form of church government, or in a capitalist social theory. It was only the intensity of their religious experience, their style of personal piety and their commitment to further religious reform that gave them a particular identity and earned them their pejorative nickname.

The emergence of nonconformity

The Prayer Book's conservative features had disappointed both the returning religious exiles who had been exposed to Reformed liturgy on the Continent and the radical Protestants who had joined underground sects during the previous reign. Some of these decided from the outset that they could not accept high ecclesiastical office in such an imperfect institution as the Elizabethan Church; for example, the Marian exile, Thomas Sampson, refused the bishopric of Ely on the grounds that: 'I cannot take upon myself the government of the church, until, after having made an entire reformation in all ecclesiastical functions, she [Elizabeth] will concede to the clergy the right of ordering all things according to the word of God.' (It has to be said, however, that his scruples did not prevent him from accepting the office of dean of Christ Church, Oxford, in 1561 (McGrath 1967).) Initially, however, most of the reformers were prepared to bide their time, convinced that the queen would allow further measures of reform, once the acute danger from the Catholics was over, and that in the meantime she and her bishops would not expect conformity to the practices they found objectionable. In the first few years of the reign, their hopes seemed justified, as the bishops tolerated considerable diversity in ceremonies and clerical dress; in Norfolk and Suffolk, for example, some sixty-four ministers did not wear the surplice or vestments during the early 1560s and yet did not incur the discipline of their bishop (MacCulloch 1986).

Only as the years passed and the queen made clear that she had no intention of modifying her settlement or allowing exceptions to the law did the initial disappointment turn to dismay. In 1563 a moderate reform package, which called for some liturgical changes, was defeated in the Lower House of Convocation by the narrowest of margins, and new procedures were immediately introduced to prevent the reformers seizing

30

the initiative again. In 1565 Elizabeth began her attack on ministers who would not conform to the ceremonies laid down in the Prayer Book. As a result, zealous Protestants had to rethink their attitude to the official Church and decide what actions to take.

Their first crisis of conscience arose over a quarrel about clerical dress. At the end of 1564 Archbishop Parker of Canterbury summoned Thomas Sampson and Lawrence Humphrey, the master of Magdalen College, Oxford, both of whom had been exiles in Switzerland during Mary's reign, to a conference to discuss their failure to wear the surplice and clerical cap and gown. On 25 January 1565 the queen intervened and widened the dispute, when she wrote a public letter to Parker which complained of 'diversity, variety, contention and vain love of singularity in her church', and urged Parker and the bishops to take instant action 'so as uniformity of order may be kept in every church'. Parker was told to ensure that ecclesiastical livings were only served by men who promised 'to observe, keep and maintain . . . order and uniformity in all the external rites and ceremonies' (Regan 1988). At this time Elizabeth was reopening negotiations for marriage with a Habsburg prince and was anxious that the outward conservatism of her Church should be displayed everywhere. Parker's response was to order a general episcopal inquiry into the lack of uniformity in ceremonies and apparel and to withhold licences to preach from clergy who refused to obey the royal regulations. The queen's letter and Parker's inquiry triggered off a serious rift within the Church, which is usually called the Vestiarian Controversy, although the dispute was not in fact primarily about vestments.

In May 1565, an example was made of Sampson, when he was deprived of his deanship by order of the queen for his intransigence in refusing to wear the surplice and outdoor clerical dress. Sampson found that his conscience would not allow him to wear clothes that would distinguish him from the laity, since he believed that it would revive the Jewish ceremonies concerning priestly dress which had been abolished by Christ but were erroneously used by idolatrous papists. Humphrey felt the same way but was saved from deprivation by the protection of Bishop Horne of Winchester, who had jurisdiction over Magdalen College. Parker's next step, in March 1566, was to issue a directive, drawn up by himself and five bishops and known as the *Advertisements*, which called for the clergy to follow 'one uniformity of rites and manners' in the administration of the sacraments and also 'one decent behaviour in their outward apparel'. In the *Advertisements* some concessions were made to the zealots, as the clergy were no longer expected to wear vestments at communion; instead, 'a comely surplice with sleeves' was prescribed. The compromise was not sufficient to satisfy some members of the London clergy, however, and in 1566 some thirty-seven London preachers were suspended from their livings for three months after refusing to conform (Collinson 1967).

The Vestiarian Controversy was a very public debate within the Church. The nonconformists used the press to put across their arguments and appealed to Bullinger and Gualter at Zurich and Beza and Guillaume Farel in Geneva for support. They tried to demonstrate that the dispute was not merely a squabble about clerical dress but a disagreement about fundamental issues concerning the nature of the reformed Church and Christian liberty.

Although Gualter and Beza gave the nonconformists some support, Bullinger pointed out that their disobedience posed a threat to the future of English Protestantism and explained that there were dangers in questioning the authority of monarchs. He urged each dissident to consider 'whether he will not more edify the church of Christ by regarding the use of habits for the sake of order and decency, as a matter of indifference' than by leaving the Church altogether and allowing it 'to be occupied hereafter if not by evident wolves, at least by ill-qualified and evil ministers'. Bullinger's words reassured the bishops who had felt uncomfortable about enforcing the drive against non-conformity. Edmund Grindal of London, John Jewel of Salisbury and James Pilkington of Durham were just three of the bishops who had sympathy with the nonconformists' cause. Like Sampson and Humphrey, they had wanted 'even the slightest vestiges of popery' to be 'removed from our churches, and above all from our minds' (John Jewel), but unlike the nonconformists they believed that these 'vestiges of popery' were matters of indifference, which could be left to the queen. If she chose to uphold them, they argued, Protestants should obey her for the sake of church unity, as dissent and disunity would only play into the hands of the papists and put at risk all that the Protestants had gained so far. Furthermore, they feared that the Puritans' refusal to obey lawful authority was leading to discussions of potentially more dangerous issues: questions about the authority of bishops and obedience to a civil magistrate, indeed about the whole area of ecclesiastical government. For these reasons the bishops aligned themselves with the queen and Parker and tried to enforce conformity and exclude the recalcitrants from places of responsibility in the Church (Collinson 1967; McGrath 1967).

In the event only a handful of the London clergy lost their licences permanently after the three months' suspension was over, but they were not silenced and they continued to preach. Spurred on by their congregations, a few of the deprived London ministers held their own private services in homes, ships and public buildings, where they preached and administered the sacrament. Their meetings could be quite large; about one hundred people attended a service at Plumbers' Hall in London, which was discovered by the sheriff's officers in June 1567. Other dissenting ministers moved to new livings where patrons turned a blind eye to their 'godly' but illegal activities and permitted or encouraged them to reject the surplice, the cross in baptism, the ring in marriage and other 'dregs of popery'. Sampson, for example, soon became master of Wigston Hospital in Leicester through the influence of the earl of Huntingdon and a prebendary of St Paul's and rector of Brightlingsea, Essex. Thus, although Elizabeth ostensibly won this first round against the Puritans, she was far from winning the fight for conformity. Protected by lay and ecclesiastical patrons, the Puritans continued to follow their conscience, to work for 'true' reformation and to protest against other popish abuses in the Church (Collinson 1967).

The Presbyterian movement

The Presbyterian movement was not a foreign import but arose as a direct result of conditions in England. Experiences of episcopal discipline during the Vestiarian Controversy embittered some of the London ministers and their supporters. They became still more aggrieved in 1571, when the ecclesiastical authorities cancelled existing licences to preach and required ministers to subscribe to the Prayer Book and Thirty-Nine Articles before new ones were issued to them. This new clampdown on Puritans resulted in the suspension and deprivation of ministers who were prepared to live with the surplice and unreformed Prayer Book but on no account would express positive approval of them. The dissidents, consequently, became still more resentful towards the bishops, grew contemptuous of their authority and began to question the scriptural basis for an episcopal Church. In this they were joined by a younger generation of clergy and academics, inspired by Calvinist teachings and disillusioned by the failure of the bishops to continue the process of reformation. These Protestants believed that a Presbyterian system of church government would lead to a preaching ministry in each parish and the establishment of a godly discipline for each congregation.

The episcopal nature of the Elizabethan Church was first criticized publicly by Thomas Cartwright, Lady Margaret Professor of Divinity at Cambridge, in his course of lectures on the first two chapters of the *Acts of the Apostles*, delivered at the University in spring 1570. The theme of the lectures was that the English Church differed in a number of fundamental respects from the Church of the New Testament and that as a consequence reforms should be made in the functions of the bishops and archdeacons. As yet, Cartwright did not present a rationale for the abolition of episcopacy, nor did he call for the establishment of a fully-fledged Calvinist system of ecclesiastical government – that was to come later. None the less, his proposals were radical enough to raise the alarm of the authorities and in December 1570 he lost his professorial chair, largely through the influence of the vice-chancellor of Cambridge, John Whitgift, later to be archbishop of Canterbury.

Cartwright's call for the institutional reform of the Church was repeated in a manifesto, published in June 1572 and known as *An Admonition to Parliament*, which was written by John Field, a minister from London suspended in 1571 or early 1572, and his colleague, Thomas Wilcox (Elton 1982). Although addressed to members of parliament, the *Admonition* was not a parliamentary petition as such but was rather an appeal to public opinion, since the authors realized that their demands were far too radical for parliament to accept. Not only did they articulate the usual grievances about 'superstitions', such as kneeling at communion, and popish practices, like the observance of holy days, but more importantly they argued for the institution of a ministry of pastors, deacons and elders to replace the existing hierarchical structure of the established Church, which in their view was ungodly and unscriptural.

In fact, this Presbyterian programme not only appalled the queen and bishops, who hastened to silence the presses, but shocked moderate Puritans as well. The latter believed that there was room for diversity of practice in ecclesiastical government, and they were anyway far more concerned with the reform of liturgy, the spread of the Word through preaching and the edification of the nation, than with the abolition of episcopacy. The older nonconformist leaders like Humphrey and Sampson kept their distance from this more radical movement, while men like Thomas Norton, who were trying to introduce parliamentary bills to reform the Prayer Book, also feared that the *Admonition* was divisive and pernicious and 'with unreasonableness and unseasonableness hath hindered much good, and done much hurt'. In consequence, hardline Presbyterianism began as, and was to remain, a marginal force within the Elizabethan Puritan movement.

For their pains, Field and Wilcox were sent to Newgate Prison for a year, but the *Admonition* was widely read. It opened up a new debate on the nature of the Church, with other writers soon joining in. Among the various pamphlets secretly published in 1572 in support of the *Admonition* and its authors was *A Second Admonition to the Parliament*, which described in greater detail a system of Presbyterian government for the Church. The *Second Admonition* may have been written by Christopher Goodman, though it was long attributed to Thomas Cartwright. A printed response to the arguments in the *Admonitions* was soon made by John Whitgift, the vice-chancellor of Cambridge responsible for the dismissal of Cartwright the previous year, and, when Cartwright printed a spirited defence of the *Admonitions* in 1573, an extended pamphlet debate followed, which served to keep the so-called Admonition Controversy in the public eye for the next two decades (Lake 1988).

The early Presbyterian leadership was based in London and Cambridge, but the movement soon began to spread out to counties as far afield as Shropshire, Norfolk and Northamptonshire through the influence of individual preachers and their ecclesiastical and lay patrons. Despite their radicalism, the early Presbyterians could count on the support and protection of powerful individuals. These were crucial to their careers and the dissemination of their ideas. Lay patronage was forthcoming mainly because committed Protestants, like the earl of Leicester and William Cecil, Lord Burghley, were deeply alarmed about the drive of the Counter-Reformation against England. During the 1570s in the wake of the papal excommunication of Eliza-beth and at a time when Catholic priests were coming to England from the seminaries on the Continent, it seemed to them a serious political mistake to silence Protestant ministers, even if they happened to be Presbyterians. This was especially true when the troublemakers were personally known to them or their kin. Thus, when Edward Dering was threatened with a suspension of his licence to preach because of his Presbyterian sympathies, he was protected from his bishop by Burghley, whose sister-in-law was his intimate friend. Similarly, when Arthur Wake was deprived by the bishop of Peterborough in 1573, Leicester warned the bishop to keep his hands off 'my loving friend' if he hoped for his support and friendship in the future. Many of the Puritan patrons were also unsympathetic to the bishops and suspected that they were acting mainly out of self-interest in repressing their critics (Collinson 1967; McGrath 1967).

Without this patronage, the Elizabethan Presbyterian move-ment would have been crushed at birth. During the time of the Admonition Controversy some of the bishops, worried about the impact of Presbyterian ideas on their status and authority, began to search out presses which published Presbyterian tracts, suspended licences to preach and in some cases threw radicals in jail. Walter Travers fled Cambridge for Geneva in 1570 to be joined later by Cartwright, who was driven into exile in 1573; John Field was silenced and may also have gone abroad. Some bishops harried not only Presbyterians but any outspoken critic or nonconformist; in London, any lay person or cleric who would not subscribe to the Prayer Book was imprisoned, and four even died from the prison conditions, 'more unwholesome than dunghills, more stinking than swine sties'. This episcopal repression exposed the lack of unity among the Presbyterians and nonconformists, since some agreed to conform and 'join hands with such bloody persecutors' to the fury of the radicals (Collinson 1967). Divisions were also obvious among those who refused to subscribe, as some took their stand on a few cere-monies while others based their objections on Presbyterian principles.

This phase of repression ended with the death of Archbishop Parker in 1575. The new incumbent at Canterbury was Edmund Grindal, who wanted to heal the divisions in the Church and to introduce reforms from above. Consequently, during his first year as archbishop, preaching was warmly encouraged and conformity was not widely enforced. Grindal, however, soon became embroiled in a heated argument with the queen over prophesyings (meetings of clergy where they practised their preaching skills and ability to use scripture). Elizabeth was convinced that prophesyings provided the radicals with the opportunity to influence other ministers, and she demanded their suppression. Grindal, however, believed that they helped to train a preaching clergy and were an indispensable tool in the evangelization of England; he consequently refused to obey the royal order. In fury at his disobedience, Elizabeth placed the archbishop under house-arrest in the spring of 1577. Although he was not deprived, Grindal was thereafter only allowed to carry out minor administrative tasks, so England was effectively left without an archbishop of Canterbury until his death in 1583.

During that time, many bishops resumed their drive against nonconformity and Presbyterianism. In dioceses such as London under Bishop Aylmer, ecclesiastical commissions were used against the radicals so successfully that their access to the pulpit was limited and their leaders had to go underground. In other areas, however, Puritan ministers could count on the active support of sympathetic gentlemen and women, and consequently episcopal attempts to impose conformity often ran into difficulties. Godly women, often widows, acted as benefactors or protectors of Puritan clergy by promoting their appointment to livings or giving them financial assistance, while godly gentlemen used their political influence more directly on behalf of their Puritan friends. For example, in 1578 the Puritan gentry of Norfolk and Suffolk used their contacts at court to sabotage Bishop Edmund Freke's attempts to suspend nonconformist preachers. Councillors like Burghley, Leicester and Sir Francis Walsingham could usually be counted upon to intervene on behalf of the Puritan gentry of East Anglia and the Midlands (MacCulloch 1986). The Catholic scare was so acute between 1579 and 1583 that these men were once again alarmed to see the bishops directing their energies against Protestant preachers when their target should have been the more dangerous crypto-papists and recusants (Catholics who did not attend the parish church). In their view, all Protestant polemicists should be used in the struggle against Rome. Thus, Burghley encouraged Walter Travers to return to England, offered him a position as chaplain in his own household and in 1581 secured for him the appointment as reader in the Temple Church. Similarly, Leicester and Sir Francis Knollys used their influence to obtain a preaching licence for John Field and a post for him as a parish lecturer at St Mary's, Aldermary in 1579 (Collinson 1967; McGrath 1967).

Thus, despite episcopal attempts to uproot Presbyterianism before 1583, the movement survived. Indeed, it appears to have continued to spread and become more organized at a grass-roots level, developing what Professor Collinson has called the Classical Movement, an organization of regional assemblies. In some parts of the country the clergy began to meet together informally, and they then started to set up regional classes or synods. The first known classis was in the village of Cockfield, in Suffolk, where in May 1582 some sixty ministers met secretly to discuss the Prayer Book, 'what might be tolerated and what necessarily to be refused in every point of it'. A little later in 1582 similar meetings are known to have taken place at Cambridge under cover of the summer graduation ceremonies, and then at Wethersfield in Essex. The best-known of the classes was the more formal series of assemblies held at Dedham, in Essex, between October 1582 and June 1589. About twenty Puritan clergy regularly attended the meetings, where issues of common concern were discussed and advice given on a wide range of problems encountered in their ministry (Collinson 1967). Most of the clergy who attended such classes were probably not committed to a Presbyterian system of ecclesiastical government but simply wanted to meet like-minded brethren to discuss the Prayer Book and reach decisions on day-to-day parochial concerns.

The Presbyterian leaders based in London, particularly John Field, had a different agenda. They recognized that the classes were a Presbyterian system in embryo, since the ministers who attended were managing their own affairs and making their own decisions without any reference to a bishop; and they thought to use the classical organization as a way of changing the nature of the Elizabethan Church from within. By encouraging the development of these model Presbyterian churches they planned to take over eventual control of the official Church. Field, therefore, helped with the organization of the Classical Movement by keeping in contact with ministers all over the country, encouraging the holding of local assemblies and arranging for a number of provincial and national synods to be held to formulate policy. He and his colleagues also tried in 1584 to mount an organized campaign to influence parliamentary elections and introduce legislation which would overturn the Elizabethan Church Settlement and replace it with a Presbyterian Church. Among their many activities, the London group held a meeting to discuss tactics for lobbying MPs and organized nation-wide petitions calling for the reform of abuses in the Church. They also began to put into action a long-term scheme to produce a nation-wide survey of the parochial clergy which would produce evidence of its deficiencies as an agent of godly reform. Finally, the Presbyterian MP Dr Peter Turner made an attempt to introduce a parliamentary bill which would provide for the establishment of a Genevan style of prayer book and a system of church government based on ministers, elders, classes and synods.

Despite their great efforts, the Presbyterians made little impact on the 1584 Parliament. Although they won some seats in boroughs with small electorates, they failed to make many gains in shires with larger electorates, even when these were Puritan strongholds like Essex and Suffolk. The House of Commons refused to read Turner's bill, and even moderate bills, such as those which aimed at removing unlearned ministers and restoring suspended clergy, were lost in the Lords thanks to the intervention of the queen.

In addition to their impotence in bringing about an official change of policy, the Presbyterians had other cause for concern in 1584. On the death of Grindal in 1583, John Whitgift, the arch-opponent of Thomas Cartwright, was appointed as archbishop of Canterbury. In his inaugural sermon at St Paul's Cross, Whitgift likened Puritans to 'Papists, Anabaptists and Rebels', and he made it his immediate priority to impose conformity on the Church. In October 1583 he issued a series of articles, which were designed to do two things: first, to remedy some of the abuses in the Church that made it vulnerable to Puritan attack; second, to stop Puritan activity by ending private meetings for worship and throwing out of the ministry anyone who refused to conform in all respects to the Prayer

Book. With this second aim in mind, Whitgift insisted that all ministers and preachers subscribe to three articles. These required them: to acknowledge the royal supremacy; to agree that the Prayer Book and the Ordinal (the ceremony to ordain ministers) contained nothing 'contrary to the word of God'; and to accept that everything in the Thirty-Nine Articles conformed to the word of God (Elton 1982).

It was the second article which created a crisis of conscience not only for Presbyterians but for many moderate Puritan ministers, who disliked aspects of the liturgy laid down in the Prayer Book and considered them to be unscriptural and ungodly. Consequently, perhaps some four hundred ministers refused to subscribe and as a result were suspended from their posts and refused licences to preach. To save their careers, however, most ministers were prepared to give a conditional subscription to the articles, even though John Field condemned qualified acceptance as 'vain and frivolous'. Whitgift himself was equally uncompromising and initially demanded total conformity to the articles. Only when he was confronted with a storm of protests from councillors and prominent royal servants about the deprivation of ministers did he back down and agree to allow a modified form of subscription, provided that the ministers undertook to use the Prayer Book. Accepting this compromise, most of the original non-subscribers signed some form of acceptance of the articles. They were often married men who would lose all means of livelihood if they stuck totally to their principles; but they could also justify their submission by arguing that they would be unable to fulfil their vocation to preach or infuse the existing Church with the spirit of true godliness if they were deprived (Collinson 1967). Had they stood firm, however, Whitgift's policy might well have failed totally; as it was, his methods were criticized in the 1584 Parliament.

Knowing that he had the full support of the queen, Whitgift was undeterred by opposition in parliament and the council. He continued to use the Court of High Commission against Puritan 'ringleaders', used new powers against the press and resisted attempts by Burghley and Leicester to promote or protect their Presbyterian protégés. George Gifford was deprived of his living despite appeals from Burghley, and Thomas Cartwright, who had recently returned to England, was refused a licence to preach when it was requested by Leicester. At the same time Whitgift continued in his task of reforming the Church in order to weaken the Presbyterian case that the existing Church was corrupt; in 1585 articles were passed in Convocation which tackled some of the grievances expressed in Puritan petitions about the state of the Church.

The Presbyterian response to Whitgift was equally confrontational. They continued to develop their organization in the country and used the press to discredit the parochial system in operation and to put forward their own proposals for reform. In 1586 they made a new onslaught in parliament. As in 1584, the Presbyterian leaders tried to influence parliamentary elections, though this time with more success, and again they held meetings to discuss tactics. This time, they also presented petitions calling for reform, which were the outcome of the surveys of the parochial clergy carried out since the summer of 1584; and a Presbyterian MP, Anthony Cope, offered to the Commons a new parliamentary bill. Cope's bill, presented in February 1587, was even more radical than that of Turner, yet the House agreed to its reading the next day, perhaps influenced by an impassioned speech by Job Throckmorton and the strong anti-Catholic feelings provoked by the revelation of the Babington Plot, an assassination plot in which Mary Stuart was implicated. The queen immediately took action to prevent the bill from proceeding further; she ordered Cope and four other MPs to the Tower and sent her spokesmen to the Commons to put the government's case against the bill. Faced with her determined refusal to allow the discussion of religion, the House caved in and did not even make a formal protest about the arrested MPs (Loach 1991).

This second parliamentary failure was disappointing but hardly unexpected. The programme contained in the bill was so radical that it was unacceptable to all moderate opinion. A more serious setback for the Presbyterians was Whitgift's muzzling of the Puritan press, which severely limited Presbyterian opportunities for positive publicity. The London-based leaders therefore decided to concentrate on developing their organization and erecting a shadow Church, a secret Presbyterian system in the country based on the *Book of Discipline* (*Disciplina Ecclesiae Sacro ex Dei Verbo Descripta*) which was written and devised by Walter Travers. As Field explained, 'Seeing we cannot compass these things by suit nor dispute, it is the multitude and people that must bring the discipline to pass which we desire' (Collinson 1967).

Field's policy was fraught with difficulty. First, its success depended upon the strength and support of the Presbyterian Classical Movement; yet, as the research of Professor Collinson has demonstrated, its organization was not spread throughout the country and the number of active members was small. In many counties there is no evidence of Presbyterian activity: Berkshire, Derbyshire, Dorset, Gloucestershire, Hampshire, Staffordshire, Wiltshire and Worcestershire as well as Wales and much of the archdiocese of York. Even where there was strong Puritan or Presbyterian influence, it was confined to pockets of a region, and its organization was mainly loose and informal. Only in Cambridge, Essex, London, Northampton-shire, Oxford, Suffolk and Warwickshire were there groups directly involved in the national movement. Second, not all members of the Classical Movement were happy with Travers's *Book of Discipline*. A number of classes would not subscribe to it, as they questioned whether all parts of it conformed to the teachings of scripture and were worried that its use might endanger 'the peace of the church'. Just as most Puritan clergy had not taken a stand against Whitgift's articles of 1583, they were unwilling to engage in revolutionary activity or to break away from the established Church.

The political conditions for embarking on this plan of action also worked against the Presbyterians. In the second half of the 1580s the Puritans found themselves dangerously isolated at court, as two anti- Puritan politicians were given more influential positions, while several of their patrons on the Council died between 1588 and 1590: in 1586 Whitgift was appointed to the Privy Council and in the following year the conformist Sir Christopher Hatton was made Lord Chancellor; Leicester died in 1588, Sir Walter Mildmay in 1589 and Sir Francis Walsing-ham and the earl of Warwick in 1590. The Presbyterians also suffered from the death in 1588 of John Field, who was irreplace-able as an organizer and leader of the national movement (MacCulloch 1990). After his death the national movement fell away; no synod was held after September 1589 and there was no Presbyterian campaign in the 1589 Parliament. The Presby-terians were weakened too by the unexpected removal of the

Catholic threat with the spectacular defeat of the Spanish Armada in 1588. Not only did the loyalty of the Catholics during this period of national emergency reduce the value of the Presbyterian ministers as a bulwark against Rome, but also belief that God had assisted his chosen people of England against the mighty forces of Anti-Christ probably convinced many that there was nothing ungodly about the English Church and no need to redesign it along Presbyterian lines.

In these circumstances, Whitgift and his associates were ready for another major assault on the Presbyterians. They were assisted in their attack by the publication of the *Marprelate Tracts*, a series of lampoons against the bishops which appeared under the pseudonym Martin Marprelate in 1588 and 1589. These scurrilous pamphlets shocked Presbyterian leaders like Cartwright and Travers and scandalized some of their patrons, who feared 'that as they shoot at Bishops now so they will do at the Nobility also, if they be suffered' (McGrath 1967). Consequently, the ecclesiastical authorities were able to exploit their appearance by portraying the Puritans as dangerous subversives and by seizing the opportunity to hunt down the Puritan presses and round up Presbyterian leaders. The man in charge of this operation was Richard Bancroft, who had been appointed a member of High Commission in 1587. His investigations led him to uncover many of the classes and synods which had been set up during the previous decade and to formulate a case against Thomas Cartwright and eight other prominent leaders of the movement. They were brought before High Commission in 1590 and Star Chamber in 1591, but they were released, partly because they conducted their defence so effectively that the case against them could not be proved and partly because they still had powerful friends at court. Their spirit was broken, however; the imprisoned leaders promised to give up their classes and synods, and neither Cartwright nor Travers (who had not been arrested) caused the episcopacy any further trouble. The Classical Movement was effectively dead.

At the same time that the bishops were winning the political struggle against Presbyterianism, they began to win the ideological debate, by developing new claims for the legitimacy of episcopal government. In the 1570s Whitgift had not argued for the divine right of episcopacy, declaring instead: 'I find no one certain and perfect kind of government prescribed or commanded in the scriptures to the church of Christ; which no doubt should have been done, if it had been a matter necessary unto the salvation of the church.' On the contrary he believed that the system of ecclesiastical government should accommodate itself to the form of government in the state and could vary according to historical circumstance. Thus, as a monarchical state England should have a system of church government such as episcopacy which allowed for the exercise of the royal supremacy, and on no account should introduce Presbyterianism, which would restrict the royal supremacy both by excluding the monarch from any role in governing the Church and by denying the Crown any right to determine its structure. During the final campaign against the Presbyterians in the late 1580s and early 1590s, however, the bishops and their supporters gained the confidence to advance a more ideological defence of their position and put forward *iure divino* (divine right) arguments in support of episcopacy. Dr John Bridges, dean of Sarum, was the first to publicize this view in his book of 1587, but he was soon followed by many others (including Richard Bancroft) who justified episcopacy on *iure divino* grounds. By the end of the reign, *iure divino* views were the new orthodoxy while Presbyterian arguments had disappeared without trace (Lake 1988).

Despite the success of the bishops in breaking the Presbyterian movement and attacking the ideology of Presbyterianism, Puritanism as a religious experience and mentality continued to thrive outside the court at the end of Elizabeth's reign. In practice nonconformity could not be eradicated while preaching, fasts and informal conferences remained an important feature of Elizabethan and Jacobean religious life in many parts of England, especially the Midlands and East Anglia. Without the distraction of political Presbyterianism, the Puritan clergy could give their undivided attention to their role as preachers and pastors. At the same time Puritan magistrates were prepared to stop attacking the unreformed features of the Elizabethan Settlement in return for freedom to further their religious ideals and consolidate their power at a local level. In this spirit, religion ceased to be a major divisive issue at both the national and the local level during the last decade of the reign (MacCulloch 1986).

6

Separatism

Separatism is a word used to label a tendency of some radical Protestants to break away from the national Church and form their own separate congregations of believers. At one time, some historians confused radical Puritans with Separatists, and saw them both as part of the same dissenting tradition. For them, there was a direct line of descent from Elizabethan Puritans, to the religious exiles on the Mayflower, down to the mid-seventeenth-century radical sects. Such historians could there-fore detect and describe many examples of Separatism in the late Elizabethan period.

Now, however, historians are defining Separatism more care-fully and they recognize that there is a narrow, but important, line dividing Elizabethan Puritans from Separatists. Unlike Separatists, Puritans remained within the national Church, attended their parish services regularly, and did not form alternative churches of the godly. Despite their dissatisfaction with the official Church and distaste for much of its liturgy and practice, most Puritans shrank away from Separatism, partly because of a fear of schism but also because they could not bring themselves to leave the fellowship of their fellow Protestants (Spufford 1974).

For Separatists, on the other hand, the blemishes in the Established Church demonstrated that it was not the 'true' Church, and they consequently felt that they had to withdraw totally from it and establish instead their own separate churches which only the elect would attend (Collinson 1983). Separatism, while distinct from Puritanism, thus took Puritanism to its logical conclusion, and many of its leaders, like Francis Johnson, a London Separatist of the early 1590s, began life as Presbyterians but gradually drifted into Separatism, as they lost hope that the Established Church would reform itself.

The roots of English Separatism can be found in the underground churches of Mary's reign and some of the London congregations which grew up during the Vestiarian Controversy. The congregation which met at Plumbers' Hall in 1567 was implicitly Separatist although few of those who attended the meetings were Separatist in intention; as their spokesmen explained to Grindal, bishop of London, they wanted to hear the godly preachers 'displaced by your law', and 'we bethought us what was best to do; and we remembered that there was a congregation of us in this city in Queen Mary's days'. Grindal, however, realized the potential sectarianism of such groups and recommended severe punishment for the ringleaders, who were in his view 'people fanatical and incurable' (Collinson 1967).

The Separatist Movement as such, however, did not take shape before the 1580s, when Robert Browne and Robert Harrison put their energies into setting up congregations of the elect and writing polemical works in support of Separatism. Both men were Cambridge graduates and deprived schoolmasters who in 1580, on deciding that 'we are to forsake and deny all ungodliness and wicked fellowship', formed a Separatist church in Norwich. Browne soon became well known to the authorities and spent some time in prison before going to Middleburg in the Netherlands with his congregation in 1582.

While abroad, Browne and Harrison published several works in which they developed a covenant theology. Their argument was that the true Church was a voluntary gathering of the godly bound by a covenant to God in separate congregations which would govern themselves. The two men, however, soon fell out and in 1583 Browne was expelled from his church, leaving Harrison in charge of the congregation at Middleburg until his death in 1585. Browne returned to England in 1584 where he made peace with Whitgift and once again took communion in the Church of England.

Despite Browne's defection, the early Separatists were known as Brownists, and groups of them continued to operate in Norwich, Essex and London during the 1580s. As the Classical Movement collapsed after 1589, Separatist activity increased in London and new leaders were found in Henry Barrow and John Greenwood, who wrote tracts from prison which were smuggled out to congregations of Separatists in England and abroad. By 1593 their activities had been discovered and the groups in London detected. New legislation was passed against 'seditious sectaries' in the parliament which met in February 1593, and Greenwood and Barrow were executed along with a leader of the London Separatists, John Penry. This draconian response to the Brownist threat seemed to work, for there is very little evidence of any further activity by Separatists in England during the rest of the reign (McGrath 1967).

Separatism in Elizabethan England was a tiny movement, thanks to the bishops' success in convincing most Puritans that the Church of England was but 'halfly reformed' rather than totally unreformed and that despite its imperfections the Church did preach the word of God (Spufford 1974). The desire for a more intense religious experience did encourage a form of semi-Separatism among Puritans as they evolved their own forms of worship and discipline, but these were not intended to be divisive nor to be cells in a separated Church. It was only when the Puritans believed in the 1630s that the bishops had moved on to the wrong theological track that Separatism mushroomed and became a threat to the ecclesiastical order.

7

Catholicism

Most historians would now agree that on the accession of Elizabeth I the majority of men and women in England and Wales were Catholic in belief. From the evidence of wills it would appear that Protestant commitment was only strong in the south-east, and that even there it still represented a minority of belief. Only 14 per cent of Sussex wills contained Protestant formulae and bequests by 1559, and no more than 10 per cent of Kent wills before 1560 had a statement of Protestant belief in the preamble. The task of the new Protestant regime of Elizabeth was, therefore, to wean the population away from its traditional beliefs and convert the country to Protestantism through preaching and education (Whiting 1989).

In this, the government had considerable success. By the end of the reign English Catholicism had shrunk to a very small sect (constituting about 1 or 2 per cent of the population), practising a household religion which posed little threat to the monarch or the Church. How and why did this change take place? Some historians argue that the die was cast in the 1560s when the conservative gentry and clerical leadership failed to mount any organized resistance to the 1559 Religious Settlement but instead allowed the ordinary laity to drift into conformity by attending Protestant church services. In the words of Patrick McGrath: 'When the parish priest was ready to use the Book of Common Prayer and the squire publicly appeared at the new services, it was hardly surprising that the ordinary people followed the examples of their social superiors.' (McGrath 1967). According to this account, it was only the later arrival of the seminary priests from Douai and the Jesuits that saved English Catholicism from extinction (Bossy 1975).

On the other hand, Christopher Haigh has recently challenged this view and placed the blame for the collapse of English Catholicism elsewhere. While he accepts that 'after they lost their monopoly of legal worship and the slow imposition of protestantism was resumed, English Catholics would, without political change, become a minority', he believes that Catholic survivalism was strong in the 1560s and that the shrinkage of the community to a tiny sect was the result of 'strategic and logistical errors' made by the seminary priests and the Jesuits (Haigh 1981 and 1984).

It is important to remember that the Catholic Church did not cave in without a struggle at the accession of Elizabeth. The clerical leadership made an early stand against the Elizabethan Settlement in the bishops' fight against the 1559 legislation in the House of Lords and in the subsequent refusal of all but one of the Marian episcopate to take the Oath of Supremacy. Many of the Catholic intelligentsia also refused to conform to the new Protestant Church. About 100 fellows and other senior members left the University of Oxford between 1559 and 1566, some to go into exile abroad. Some academics went to the Catholic University of Louvain, from where they published more than forty books and pamphlets between 1564 and 1568: polemical works, theological treatises, devotional guides and books on the development of the Christian life. By 1564 Louvainist attacks on the Elizabethan Church were being smuggled into England, and by 1566 the queen was so concerned about the illicit importation of foreign works that she recommended boats be searched for Catholic books (McGrath 1967).

Only a small proportion of parish priests followed the example of their bishops. Perhaps some 300 of the Marian clergy were deprived of their livings for refusing to take the Oath of Supremacy, between 70 and 80 went into exile, and at least 130 suffered terms of imprisonment at one time or another, including 30 or so who died in prison. (McGrath 1984 and 1989). This was a small percentage of the total, to be sure, but their influence was greater than their numbers might suggest, as many of the deprived clergy worked as private tutors in gentry households and offered Catholic sacraments in private chapels or their own homes. In the 1560s over 150 deprived Marian priests were active in Yorkshire and 75 in Lancashire, offering masses, baptisms and churchings, celebrating prohibited feasts and hearing confessions. Smaller numbers were working too in the dioceses of Chichester, Durham, Hereford, Lichfield, Peterborough, Winchester and Worcester. Through their work, semi-recusant and recusant groups existed throughout the country by the early 1570s, well before the seminary priests from Douai had arrived to make any impact on the Catholic community. Between 1569 and 1570 132 recusants were found in Hampshire, while Bishop Parkhurst's visitation of the archdeaconry of Norwich uncovered 180 recusants (Haigh 1981).

Although the Pope was certainly slow to act against Elizabeth and gave no spiritual guidance to the Catholics in 1559, there were some papal attempts to encourage recusancy in the 1560s. In 1562 the Council of Trent made a general statement that Catholics should not attend Protestant church services; in 1564 a committee of the Council declared specifically that English Catholics should stay away from their churches; and in 1566 the newly elected Pope Pius V forbade church attendance and sent Lawrence Vaux, the deprived master of Manchester College, as his envoy to England to inform Catholics of this decision. Although the mission had little practical success, his example was soon followed by a number of Louvainists who encouraged English Catholics to refuse attendance at church. Consequently, there existed in England from 1566 onwards the concept of a separated Catholic Church united with Rome, with some individuals and communities moving slowly towards making that idea a reality.

Of the Marian priests who stayed in their posts, not all meekly conformed to Protestantism; perhaps only a handful expressed to their flocks their contempt for the new Protestant Prayer Book, but many others kept alive a variety of Catholic rituals and practices within the parish church. Episcopal visitations and church-wardens' accounts from all parts of the country demonstrate that some churches retained their Catholic altars, rosary beads and holy water, while their priests continued to say masses for the dead, revere images and 'counterfeit' the mass in the communion services. Catholic survivalism of this

kind was strongest in the north of England, especially Lancashire, and in Wales, but there were pockets of Catholicism
sustained by the Marian priests in many other counties during
the 1560s, including the later Puritan strongholds of Norfolk
and Suffolk (Duffy 1992; Haigh 1981).

The government was well aware of this situation, as bishops
frequently complained about the presence of church papists and
recusant priests in their dioceses. Bishop John Scory of Hereford
reported in 1564 that Marian priests who 'be mortal and deadly
enemies to this religion' were holding masses in their houses and
'deriding and mocking this religion and the ministers thereof';
Bishop Sandys of Worcester reported in 1569 that 'The fruits of
my travail are counterfeited countenances and hollow hearts';
and in the same year Bishop Barlow of Chichester wrote to the
government of the 'popish ornaments' and 'old popish Latin
primers' that were still being used in the town of Battle and
other places in his diocese (Regan 1988).

The government found it difficult, however, to tackle the
problem in the 1560s. In order to avoid inciting rebellion or a
foreign crusade, the queen preferred to employ persuasion rather
than coercion against her Catholic subjects, even though there
were insufficient Protestant ministers to preach the Word and
convert the Catholic populace. Quite reasonably, she expected
Catholicism to wither away as the older generation of Catholics
died off and the supply of priests dried up. She also appreciated
that coercion would be ineffective, since her bishops did not
have the resources to root out Catholicism in parts of the
country like Yorkshire where some 75 per cent of the leading
families were Catholic. Consequently, the queen and her servants usually only took vigorous action against individuals
when they openly defied the law. Thus, Catholics attending
mass at the houses of the French and Spanish ambassadors in
London were arrested after fairly regular raids at Easter and on
feast days. Examples were made of prominent men and women
believed to be Catholic sympathizers; Lady Hobblethorne of
Essex and Lady Cary and Sir Thomas Stradling of Glamorgan-
shire all spent time in prison during the early 1560s. On the
other hand, despite some purges Catholics and their sympathizers continued to serve on the bench of magistrates and as
church-wardens, even though they would protect recusants or
their fellow church papists; similarly, Catholic lords sat on the

Privy Council and in the House of Lords and acted as lords lieutenant in the counties. There were, moreover, no martyrs to the Catholic cause; even the deprived bishops did not receive the death penalty or end their days in the Tower. Elizabeth circumvented the 1563 legislation which imposed the death penalty on anyone who twice refused the Oath of Supremacy by instructing Archbishop Parker not to offer it more than once. Punishments meted out for lesser offences were extremely lenient by Tudor standards; church-wardens at Aysgarth, for example, were sentenced to attend the service 'bare-headed, bare-footed and bare-legged', and to make a public confession for hiding certain images and 'old papistical books' (Duffy 1992; McGrath 1967 and 1989).

While in the short term the government's avoidance of confrontation with the Catholics allowed Catholicism to survive throughout the country during the 1560s, in the longer term it helped to ensure its eventual failure, as few felt pressured into recusancy or rebellion before 1569. As a result the Elizabethan regime had time to establish itself, accustom many men and women to the new Church and win over the conservative landowners. Similarly, although the work of the Marian priests who 'counterfeited the mass' in the parish church certainly aided the survival of Catholicism in the first decade of Elizabeth's reign, it also probably assisted the Protestant Church in the longer term. By staying in their livings, the Marian priests rescued the Protestant Church from a manpower crisis, for if more clergy had been deprived for refusing the Oath of Supremacy, it is unlikely that they could have been easily replaced, and many parishes would have been left with no spiritual care whatsoever. Furthermore, by preserving some outward forms of Catholicism, the Marian priests helped conservative parishioners make the transition from the old religion to the new more easily than would have been possible if they had been confronted with a zealous Protestant minister determined to stamp out all signs of papistry and 'superstition'. As a consequence few Catholics felt the need to separate from the established Church in the 1560s, and many slipped into conformity or conversion.

Despite the work of the Marian priests and the beginnings of recusancy, lay commitment to most forms of Catholic devotion appears to have been in decline in many areas of England by the early 1570s. Evidence from the ecclesiastical courts in the diocese of Exeter and the ecclesiastical commission at York demonstrates that fewer cases concerning 'superstitious' ceremonies and the retention of images were being reported to the authorities in the early 1570s than there had been a decade earlier. In the words of Dr Whiting, the historian of the south-west during the Reformation: 'by 1570 no more than a relatively limited minority of the English people could have been meaningfully classified as committed Catholics' (Whiting 1989).

None the less, just as their numbers were probably diminishing, Catholics were increasingly being perceived as a threat to the security of the realm, largely because of changes in the political situation in England and abroad. Deteriorating relations with Spain after 1568 and Mary Stuart's flight to England in the same year to seek refuge from her rebellious subjects raised the spectre of Catholic plots and conspiracies at home supported by Spanish military power. The election in 1566 of Pope Pius V, who soon after his elevation referred to Elizabeth publicly as one 'who pretended to be queen of England', raised anxieties that he would soon call for a crusade to depose Elizabeth. Fears of the Catholic threat seemed vindicated when the Northern Rebellion broke out in 1569, the Pope issued *Regnans in Excelsis* (the bull excommunicating and deposing Elizabeth) in 1570, and the Ridolfi Plot was discovered in 1571. In 1572 the massacre of the French Huguenots on St Bartholomew's Day convinced many that there was an international plot to wipe out Protestantism throughout Europe.

In reality, however, the danger from English Catholics was exaggerated. The vast majority of them were loyal to their queen and country and simply hoped for better times when the Catholic Mary Stuart would succeed to the throne. The Northern Rebellion was largely contained within the northern counties of Durham, Northumberland, Westmorland and Yorkshire, and there was no sign of Catholic revolt in counties like Hampshire where Catholicism was strong during these troubled years. Only two Catholic polemicists, John Leslie and Nicholas Sanders, wrote books expressing political opposition to the Elizabethan government; other English Catholic leaders, including William Allen, publicly urged Catholics to ignore the papal bull (Holmes 1982).

The government responded to the crises of 1569 to 1572 by

putting greater pressure on the Catholics. More inquiries were held into recusancy, and the Privy Council ordered new groups of people to subscribe to the supremacy and Prayer Book. JPs had to sign statements that they accepted the liturgy of the Established Church, lawyers at the Inns of Court were questioned about their attendance at communion and many bishops took firmer action against recusants. Those detected as Catholics were usually fined, some lawyers were expelled from their Inn and some lost their position on the bench of magistrates. Arrests were also made, and so many ended up in jails scattered around the country that plans were made in 1572 to establish a special prison for Catholics at Wisbech, on the Isle of Ely, in the hope that they would not in the future 'corrupt others in stubbornness'. Only those considered traitors were executed, though this included not just rebels but those who had gravely offended the government, men like James Felton who pinned the papal Bull of Excommunication on the gate of the bishop of London's palace and was put to death in 1570. In 1571 new legislation was passed which prohibited the import of bulls and any other instruments from the see of Rome (which included crosses and pictures) on a charge of praemunire, which was punishable by death. It was thus extremely dangerous for anyone in England to have any contact at all with the Pope; but parliamentary attempts to impose tougher fines for recusancy and to enforce the taking of communion at least once a year were vetoed by Elizabeth, who insisted that she would introduce no inquisition to look into her subjects' souls (McGrath 1967).

By 1574 the crisis seemed over, and the government appeared to be in a more confident frame of mind about the Catholic threat. In that year, however, the first priests began to trickle over from Douai in the Spanish Netherlands to sustain the Catholic community in England. The seminary at Douai had been established in 1568 by William Allen – one of the Oxford exiles who had gone to Louvain – as an educational centre for English youths, but it soon became a training place for secular priests (clerics who did not belong to a religious order) who would embark on missionary work in England. The aim of the college was not to provide its students with polemical tools which could be used in the work of conversion but to turn out pastors who would administer the sacraments and provide spiritual guidance to Catholics who had fallen into schism. In

1573 the first students were ordained and in 1574 four Douai priests came to England, to be followed by seven in 1575, eighteen in 1576 and fifteen in 1577. By 1580 about one hundred priests had come to England, and in that year the first Jesuits also began to arrive from the English College at Rome, which had been founded in 1578. The number of Jesuits in England under Elizabeth was probably never more than four at any one time in the 1580s and rarely more than twelve in the 1590s, in contrast with the secular priests who numbered between 120 and 150 in any one year during the same periods (McGrath 1989; Bossy 1975). Despite the paucity of their numbers, the influence of all these priests was great, for they encouraged many gentry families to become or remain recusant at a time when Catholics were defecting to Protestantism.

During the 1570s and 1580s the drift towards Protestantism could not be contained by the Catholic priests. Nor could they prevent the occasional or regular acts of conformity by more committed Catholics. Sometimes only the head of a household would conform while other members of his family continued to hear mass at home. In some cases, whole families conformed, if only superficially, worn down as they were by the difficulties of sustaining their religion in the face of persecution and the state's refusal to recognize marriages or baptisms not performed by a Protestant minister. The shortage of priests made it impossible for some to receive the sacraments, the life-blood of their faith, while the lack of a Catholic education deprived most lay people of an intellectual understanding of their beliefs, which made them vulnerable to the arguments of a university-trained Protestant preacher. The exact numbers who conformed are unknown, but reports from most parts of the realm suggest that year by year individuals and small groups of Catholic gentry families were joining the Protestant Church from the mid-1580s onwards, while popular Catholicism all but died out (Wark 1971; Aveling 1980; Hilton 1977).

At the same time, however, recorded incidents of recusancy actually increased in many areas. It appears that a polarization process was going on, and as one section of conservatives was becoming Protestant, another was becoming fully committed to the Catholic religion. Due to the targeting of the missionary priests, a disproportionately large group of these recusants were members of gentry families, who were often related to each other by blood and marriage and connected by ties of friendship, while a significant number were women. Two-thirds of the 300 Catholic recusant households in Yorkshire between 1580 and 1603 were gentry, and at least thirty-five were led by women whose husbands had conformed. In Cheshire, just over a third of known recusants between 1594 and 1603 were from the gentry, and rather more than half were women (Wark 1971; Aveling 1980).

Not surprisingly, the government was horrified by the arrival of the missionaries from the Continent. At one level, they were seen as the agents of Anti-Christ, a threat to true religion, and at another as a political danger. At the very least they were encouraging Catholics to break the law on religion while at worst they appeared to be a fifth column for Elizabeth's enemies abroad. Most of the queen's councillors believed the worst and were determined to hunt down and punish the priests and their harbourers. Consequently, more consistent action was taken against the Catholic community after 1575. Prominent Catholics were placed under close surveillance by bishops, magistrates and paid informers; their activities were reported to the Privy Council; those found suspicious were detained for questioning and both persuasion and threats were employed to make them conform. Those who remained firm in their recusancy were heavily fined, arrested or confined to designated parts of the country, but they were very rarely treated as traitors and put to death. Legislation of 1585 did make it a felony punishable by death to give a priest aid, refuge or comfort, but the law was applied only erratically. In all, 63 lay people have been recognized as martyrs by the Catholic Church, although another 71 men and 27 women are known to have died in prison. By contrast, a high proportion of priests were tortured and put to death as traitors unless they conformed. The first to be hanged, drawn and quartered was Cuthbert Mayne, in 1577, who was found in possession of an agnus dei (a Catholic talisman) and a papal bull. Slightly more than 20 per cent of the priests sent to England suffered a similar fate. Of the approximately 650 priests working in England during Elizabeth's reign, 133 were executed and at least 377 spent time in prison, with about 30 of them confined to prison for over ten years (McGrath 1989).

Despite the more intense persecution of their religion in the 1580s, most lay Catholics remained loyal to the queen. Very few resorted to plots against her life or, at a local level, reacted with violence against those enforcing the penal laws. The vast majority continued to await better times when Catholicism might be restored under the Stuarts or when they might be granted toleration by a Protestant regime. They accepted passively the penalties for recusancy or tried to evade them by seeking the support of important Protestants, like the earl of Essex or Sir Robert Cecil, who sometimes intervened on their behalf. Several prominent Catholics stressed their loyalty to the queen in statements and petitions, not always produced under duress. In 1585 a group of Catholic nobles and gentry led by Sir Thomas Tresham presented Elizabeth with a petition stating that Catholics owed obedience to her, their lawful monarch, and denying that the Pope had power to authorize the 'false, devilish and abominable' act of regicide. One Catholic author concluded his moving account of the death of the Jesuit Edmund Campion with a poem which included the stanza:

God save Elizabeth our Queen
God send her happy reign
And after early honours here
The heavenly joys to gain.
              (Holmes 1982)

Even after 1581, when the priests' leaders, William Allen and Robert Parsons, had begun to call for the restoration of Catholicism by force and urged the foreign invasion of England, there was very little Catholic support for the Spanish Armada in 1588. On the contrary, some expressed publicly their loyalty to the queen, while recusants incarcerated in the bishop of Ely's palace begged to be given leave to fight for their country. Such political loyalism was only possible because of the nature of the Elizabethan persecution. Although Catholics faced heavy punishments, economic difficulties and political harassment, unlike the French Huguenots they were never as a group confronted with a threat to their very survival, nor did they as individuals face total economic ruin if they continued in their faith. The queen wanted to push them into conformity not to persecute them, to milk them of money but not to reduce them to such penury that they might become a charge on the community or be forced to rebel. By 1586 the Privy Council was beginning to recognize that recusancy could not be eliminated, only controlled, and that a religious minority could be a permanent source of income.

Despite the Allen–Parsons call to arms and the intense persecution they faced, most of the seminary priests also opposed the withdrawal of obedience from Elizabeth. In 1580 Gregory XIII had told the missionaries that the 1570 bull did not bind English Catholics to disobey their monarch in the present circumstances, and he instructed the priests to stay clear of politics. In general they obeyed his instructions, and the Jesuits too did not stir up rebellion. The Jesuit Robert Southwell wrote to Elizabeth, probably in 1591, that 'our religion, ... more than any other, tieth us to a most exact submission to your temporal authority, and to all points of allegiance'. During the Archpriest Controversy of 1598 (see p. 61) a group of the secular priests (known as the Appellants) publicly and explicitly refuted the principle that the Pope had any power over princes in temporal affairs and denied too that Catholicism might rightly be spread by force. They therefore wanted the Catholic powers to abandon their political and military pressure on the queen, and the English Catholics to work for some degree of religious toleration (Holmes 1982; Pritchard 1979).

The role of the seminary priests in the history of post-Reformation Catholicism is a matter of dispute among historians today. John Bossy has claimed that the seminary priests rescued English Catholicism from extinction and created a new post-Reformation Catholic community which owed a great deal to continental influences (Bossy 1975). In response, Dr Haigh argues that the influence of the foreign-trained priests on the growth of recusancy has been greatly exaggerated, that the mission brought nothing new to English Catholicism and that its 'strategic and logistical errors' turned the existing Catholic groups throughout the country into a rump community largely confined to gentry families in the north (Haigh 1981 and 1984).

As already seen, Dr Haigh is certainly right to point out that recusancy predated the arrival of the seminary priests. There is also considerable evidence in support of his view that there was continuity between the traditionalist communities of the 1560s and the recusants of the late 1570s and 1580s. In Cheshire, apart from the city of Chester, recusancy was largely centred on the villages of Bunbury and Malpas in the south-west, where two Marian priests had been active in the 1560s. In the dioceses of Chichester and Exeter, men reported as opponents of the Protestant Church in 1564 were recusants in 1577. There was often continuity too between harbourers of priests in the 1560s and 1580s; for instance, Thomas Westby of Moorbridge Hall, Lancashire, who had been sheltering a Marian priest in 1568 was found harbouring a seminary priest in 1582. In practically every area of England, wherever the bishops had difficulty in enforcing the Prayer Book in the 1560s, there were substantial numbers of recusants by the late 1570s: south-east Hampshire, Herefordshire, south and west Lancashire, west Sussex, south Wales, Worcestershire, the Derbyshire Peaks and the northern edges of both the North Riding and West Riding (Wark 1971; Haigh 1981; McGrath 1989).

At the same time, Dr Haigh has convincingly shown that the clergy trained abroad did not bring with them a new Counter-Reformation form of Catholicism. The movement towards an inner spirituality and a separatist household religion, which Professor Bossy attributed to their influence, had already begun among many Catholic families as their particular response to the advance of Protestantism; and in any event a seigneurial religion (based around a gentry or noble household) was not the only model of Catholic life experienced after 1580, as Dr Aveling has shown in his study of Yorkshire Catholic households (Aveling 1980). Furthermore, the seminary priests had no training in a new form of Catholicism, since their intended role in England was to provide pastoral care for a pre-existing Catholicism. Even in their emphasis on the importance of loyalty to Rome, the seminary priests and Jesuits were adding little that was new; until the 1590s they studiously avoided discussing the nature of the papal supremacy and throughout their time in England they generally followed the approach of those Marian priests who had refused to take the Oath of Supremacy yet made a strong defence of political non-resistance.

Dr Haigh's argument is less convincing, however, when he blames the seminary priests for the failure of the mission to keep Catholicism alive in all parts of the country. He is certainly right to stress some of the mistakes made by the priests which limited the effectiveness of their work, if only to counteract the hagiographical accounts which have dominated the historical writings on their mission. It is true that too many of the priests concentrated their efforts on the south and east rather than spreading further afield to regions where there were more recusants and greater Catholic potential. In 1580 only one-fifth of the missionary priests were active in the north which had two-fifths of detected recusants, whereas half were in the south-east, which had but a fifth. Yet this disparity in resources was not because of some sort of 'martyr cult' among the priests who chose to live near London where they were more likely to be captured, nor because they preferred the comfort of life in the south. It was the result of both geography and politics. Priests who left the Continent via Dieppe, Calais or Dunkirk landed on the south coast of England and naturally made for London or the Home Counties. London also acted as a magnet for the priests because of the Catholic communications network established there, as well as the perception that a presence in the capital was essential if English Catholicism was to have a national organization and a political future.

Similarly, Dr Haigh is too harsh in criticizing the mission for its excessive reliance on gentry support: 'The gentlemen have been credited with ensuring 'the survival of the faith' – and so they did, but their faith, at the expense of everyone else's' (Haigh 1981). It is true that the gentry were usually prepared to be more accommodating to the authorities than some of the priests, especially the Jesuits, would have liked. Their timidity led to the increase in occasional conformity and an unwillingness to allow the priests to proselytize among the lower orders which helped bring about the stagnation of the Catholic community in the 1590s. Furthermore, without a strong popular basis of support, the community, dominated by interrelated gentry families, became rather introverted and fossilized. None the less, Haigh's criticism is less than fair. The co-operation of the gentry was crucial to the survival of Catholicism. Gentry money, shelter and social contacts supported the work of the priests and gave them protection against the authorities. Without them and their network of safe houses it is difficult to see how the mission could have continued in the face of governmental persecution, except in the most remote areas of the country. The priests' decision to address their mission to the gentry is understandable too, and was not the result of a preference for the easy life of a chaplain in a manor-house over the uncomfortable one of a missionary working with the poor, as Haigh implies. In a hierarchical society it made far more sense to target the leaders of a community, who would then influence their tenants and dependants. As John Gerard wrote: 'The way, I think, to go about making converts is to bring the gentry over first and then their servants, for Catholic gentlefolk must have Catholic servants.' Moreover, once the parish churches had Protestant ministers and could no longer be used as places for traditional worship, the private chapel in a manor-house seemed a natural alternative as a centre of Catholic life.

On the other hand, the priests do deserve some criticism for allowing bitter squabbles to develop in their midst, which distracted them from their task of mounting a united assault on Protestantism and played into the hands of the English government. Open disagreements first broke out in the early 1590s among the inmates of the castle at Wisbech where Catholics were confined from 1579 onwards. While part of the trouble lay in personal grudges between the leading protagonists, also of importance was the rivalry between the secular priests and the Jesuits. This rivalry surfaced again in 1598 when the Pope agreed to accept a Jesuit proposal to appoint an archpriest for England who would have authority over all the secular priests trained in the seminaries, and especially when the man appointed was George Blackwell, a known admirer of the Jesuit mission. Many of the secular priests suspected that Blackwell was a puppet of the Jesuits and would work to put the vastly more numerous seculars under their control. Determined to keep their independence, some of the secular priests' leaders refused to accept Blackwell's authority and appealed to the Pope against his appointment, hence earning the name 'the Appellants' (Pritchard 1979).

The dispute became known as 'the Archpriest Controversy' and blew up into a bitter polemical debate between the Jesuit leaders and the Appellants, which led to violent quarrels within the English clergy. It only ended in 1602 when Pope Clement VIII agreed to make some concessions to the Appellants, most notably that the Archpriest should not consult or co-operate with the Jesuits in carrying out his duties. In the meantime, however, some of the Appellants had approached the English government, in the hope of persuading the queen to agree to a measure of toleration for Catholics who were politically loyal in return for the withdrawal of the Jesuits from England. The government decided to back the Appellants, both in order to encourage dissension among the Catholics and to rout the Jesuits, who were viewed as the militant allies of Spain, but the queen had no serious intention of granting any religious toleration. In 1602 she issued a proclamation which accused the Appellants of 'disloyalty and disobedience', though it refrained from describing them as traitors, and which offered her mercy to any secular priests who gave themselves up to the authorities and publicly acknowledged their allegiance to her. Not surprisingly, very few priests took advantage of this offer, and the majority also opposed an idea of the Privy Council that the priests would be given immunity from the penal laws only if they stopped practising as priests. A small group of Appellant priests, however, did sign a protestation of allegiance to the queen in January 1603, which asserted that they were morally bound to resist Catholic attempts to depose her, even though they owed the Pope obedience in spiritual matters: 'For, as we are most ready to spend our blood in the defence of her Majesty and our country, so we will rather lose our lives than infringe the lawful authority of Christ's Catholic church.' This declaration was both unacceptable to the government because it asserted the papal supremacy and disliked by others within the mission who refused to sign it. Not only was the Archpriest Controversy, therefore, conducted with a bitterness and invective which poisoned relationships; it also uncovered important differences of principle among the priests. The antagonisms and ill-feelings engendered by the dispute continued well into the seventeenth century.

Whatever their mistakes and weaknesses, the contribution of both the Jesuits and the secular priests to the survival of English Catholicism as a viable community should not be underplayed by historians. As Dr Haigh himself reluctantly admits, it is difficult to see how Catholicism could have continued in England for much longer after 1574 without an infusion of foreign-trained priests to administer the sacraments. Certainly it failed to survive in areas such as north-west Wales, the Cheviots, Cornwall, Cumberland or Westmorland where it had been strong in the 1560s but where the seminary priests failed to penetrate in the 1580s (Hilton 1980). There can also be little doubt that the heroism and spiritual guidance of the priests encouraged some Catholics to withdraw totally from their parish church and stiffened the resolve of others to remain recusants. Through their influence, there was a considerable expansion of recusancy in many northern regions after 1578, and a dramatic increase in London and Middlesex in the 1590s (though it may be, of course, that the recorded numbers of recusants are inflated by the increased number of governmental searches for Catholics).

The Jesuits also gradually developed a communications system for the whole English mission. Robert Parsons established lines of communication through France into England by 1584, and William Weston raised a fund to support the mission in 1585 and in the following year developed a network of safe houses in the country. Henry Garnet supervised this system for the next twenty years, with the help of Robert Southwell and John Gerard until their capture in the 1590s; their establishment of a shelter in London to aid new arrivals and their improvement of the regional organization probably helped save many priests from arrest and death.

In conclusion, it was not the failure of the Catholic leadership in the 1560s that doomed Catholicism to decline under Elizabeth I; on the contrary, the Marian priests helped Catholicism to survive the first decade of the reign in reasonable shape. Nor was it the fault of the seminary priests that the Catholic community was reduced to a small minority sect by 1603; despite the weaknesses of their mission, it is difficult to see how without their input Catholicism could have survived into the next century as anything other than the superstitious rituals of backward communities. In reality, given the long reign of Elizabeth and the certainty of a Protestant successor after Mary, Queen of Scots' execution in 1587, the decline of Catholicism was a gradual but inevitable process. The long and remorseless governmental persecutions and the slow but sustained exposure to Protestantism weaned most Catholics from their faith; only the most committed became recusants; the vast majority drifted into conformity and their children or grandchildren became Protestants.

8

Assessment: strengths and weaknesses of the Elizabethan Church

According to Puritan complaint literature, the Elizabethan Church was in very poor shape indeed: the laity lacked a basic understanding of Protestant doctrines and was ungodly in its behaviour; the clergy was poorly educated and unable to preach; and institutions like the church courts were unreformed and corrupt.

While it is true that the Puritans held impossibly high standards of what they considered to be a 'true' and 'godly' Church, they did have some good reasons to be gloomy in their assessment of the state of religion, particularly during the first half of Elizabeth's reign. During the 1560s there was much to be done in the work of conversion, yet there existed only a tiny Protestant preaching ministry to carry out the task. Partly as a result of a mortality crisis in the late 1550s, there was a dire shortage of clergy in the early Elizabethan Church, and vacant livings had to be hurriedly filled with poorly qualified men, who lacked the knowledge and skills necessary to proselytize effectively. Furthermore, as already seen, many parishes continued to be served by Marian priests who did their utmost to frustrate the spread of Protestant beliefs and worship as laid down in the 1559 Prayer Book. These clergymen did not die off as quickly as perhaps the Protestant establishment would have liked and many lingered on into the mid-1570s and beyond, holding up the work of reform.

At the same time the laity was resistant to change. Church-wardens were slow to comply with the law and rid the churches of Catholic plate, vestments, altars and images, not just in the more conservative north but also in southern parishes such as Great St Mary's Cambridge and St Edmund's Salisbury, where such items were not sold off until 1568. Despite the efforts of bishops, village communities also clung on to Catholic rituals and festivities, such as ringing bells on All Souls' Eve and participating in supplicatory processions and 'charming of fields' at Rogationtide (Duffy 1992).

Even at the end of the reign the work of Reformation was incomplete. Ordinary men and women were ignorant about the finer points of Protestant doctrine, and many continued to believe that good deeds played some role in their own salvation. Thomas Cartwright was probably correct in his observation that 'heaps' of people had cast away the old religion without discovering the new (Haigh 1984). Not only did they not understand predestinarianism but they also could not be weaned easily from their reliance on supernatural forces at times of stress. Bereft of the intercession of their priest, the Virgin Mary and the Catholic saints, many villagers resorted to charms, talismans and the magical powers of cunning men and women to see them through difficult times.

At the same time, the administration of the Church was barely reformed in Elizabeth's reign, and many Protestants (and not just Puritans) were dismayed that opportunities had not been taken to overhaul the church courts and bishoprics, as well as to end pluralism and absenteeism in the parishes. Historians can also point to other weaknesses in the post-Reformation Church, not least the extreme inequalities in the value of individual livings so that several thousand vicars had difficulty in support-ing their families while other ministers could live like minor gentry. Radical reforms were impossible to achieve, however, in all these areas, as too many vested interests were at stake and there was little agreement about the form of reform that should be undertaken.

For these reasons and more, the state of religion in Eliza-bethan England fell short of the Puritan ideal. None the less, historians should not underestimate the achievements of the late Elizabethan Church: the great advance made in the con-version of the people during the second half of the reign, the improvement in the quality of the clergy and the revitalization of the church courts.

Through the efforts of the government, bishops and Puritan laity, a new framework for Protestant worship and devotion was erected in most English parishes, which ultimately led to a major change in religious beliefs. Lay people's memory of Catholic forms of worship gradually disappeared as the external features of the old religion were eventually removed from the churches, while a regular exposure to the Elizabethan Prayer Book and to Protestant sermons imbued ordinary men and women with a deep anti-papalism, a strong iconophobia (hatred of images) and a growing affection for the liturgy of the Protestant service. As a result, a significant growth in Protestant feeling can be detected in most regions of England after 1570 from a range of sources. The preambles of wills (despite their limitations as source-material) point to a decisive shift from belief in the Holy Virgin and 'holy company of saints' to a 'personal faith in the mediation of Christ and redemption through Him' (Spufford 1974). Church-wardens' accounts also document the victory of the Protestant religion over traditional beliefs in thousands of parishes; just to take the example of one parish, the records of Morebath, in Devon, trace the steps of a conservative priest in a conservative parish, from holding a fervent belief in the cult of the saints and keenly supporting the Marian restoration in 1553 to becoming a minister who could register in 1573 his joy in the gift to his church of a communion book and psalter for the Protestant service (Duffy 1992). Finally, court records suggest that the laity was showing a greater readiness to attend church regularly during the last years of the reign, which presumably indicated its acceptance of the Protestant message in the sermon and liturgy, and they also record very few cases of gross irreverence such as spitting, heckling or snoring (Ingram 1987). With all this evidence before us, it is reasonable to describe England by 1603 as 'undoubtedly a Protestant nation', despite the continuance of superstitions and the rudimentary understanding of doctrines (Doran and Durston 1991).

Although the change in the patterns of belief initially owed much to coercion, as ecclesiastical commissions and church courts enforced attendance at church and attacked the survival of Catholic practices, preachers increasingly played an important role in the work of conversion. In the second half of the reign, preaching was to become a regular feature of life in many English market towns and villages and helped to form a Protestant mentality as well as to convince many people of the errors of the papal past; as two colliers from a mining community in Derbyshire explained in 1575, they had been 'ignorant and obstinate papists' until a new preacher had led them 'to a comfortable feeling of their salvation in Christ'. Their experience, though impossible to quantify, was by no means unique (Haigh 1984).

Widespread preaching was not provided by the government but came about through the efforts of committed individuals who funded local lectureships to increase the provision of sermons, endowed the two new university colleges of Emmanuel and Sidney Sussex, Cambridge, to train 'godly' ministers, and used their patronage to place trained preachers in livings under their control (Collinson 1982). A change in expectations also encouraged prospective clergy to have a university education, especially after 1575 when a regulation was passed which made 23 the minimum age for ordaining deacons (the lowest rung on the clerical career ladder). The effect of these piecemeal initiatives was a slow, but none the less dramatic, improvement in the educational qualifications and preaching abilities of the clergy. From 1575 until the Civil War, England was making steady progress towards the reality of an all-graduate clergy for its parish ministry (O'Day 1979). In the meantime, men with a licence to preach gave sermons on weekdays in local market towns, so that there was no shortage of preaching in late-Elizabethan England (Collinson 1982).

While the presence of a well-trained clergy was important for the task of evangelization and a sign of a reformed Church, it none the less created new problems by separating and perhaps alienating the graduate minister from his parishioners. In some rural parishes his sermons were little understood and frankly boring, while in others his high moral stand could lead to resentment and communal strife. Thanks to his graduate status, he was placed on a social rank higher than most of his parishioners and was given the new honorific title of 'Master', instead of being referred to by his Christian name prefixed with 'Sir'.

Because of this, the historian Christopher Haigh has argued

that the post-Reformation clergyman was more unpopular than his late-medieval counterpart and that anticlericalism developed in England as a result of the Reformation (Haigh 1977). The evidence Dr Haigh produces of resentment towards the clergy, however, is both partial and inadequate, for not only is it clear that the clergy was engaged in pastoral work which brought them into close personal contact with their parishioners but also the records provide examples of positive lay sentiments towards the local minister. Many ministers acted as schoolteachers instructing the young in the catechism, gave comfort at the sickbed and the funeral service, and tried to arbitrate between quarrelling neighbours to restore harmony to their communities. Positive appreciation for their work can be seen in wills, where legacies were sometimes left to ministers and bequests often made towards the upkeep of the parish church (Ingram 1987). While some communities may have felt resentment towards the clergy, therefore, others were satisfied with its role and some even developed close bonds with their minister.

Lay use of the church courts also indicates a satisfaction with the Elizabethan Church rather than the anticlericalism suggested by Dr Haigh. Recent studies of the working of the ecclesiastical courts have revealed that lay communities shared the clergy's concern over non-attendance at church, all forms of sexual immorality and disputes over defamation of character, and that they consequently co-operated with the courts in helping to detect and prosecute offenders. Even defendants in disciplinary cases showed their respect for the courts by turning up to answer charges against them and by obeying court orders. According to a study of the courts in Wiltshire, the record of non-attendance at ecclesiastical courts was little different from that at secular courts, and those who failed to attend were usually the young and footloose who were in trouble for sexual offences and had fled the parish when their partner had fallen pregnant. Overall, then, the church courts were working effectively at the end of the Elizabethan period and had survived the mid-Tudor years with renewed confidence and vitality.

Through both their work in the church courts and their influence as preachers, the late Elizabethan clergy played an important role in setting the social and moral standards of the community. Some historians would even argue that some early-modern sexual mores began to change under their pressure: for example, according to Dr Ingram, the clergy's insistence that all marriages had to be solemnized and sanctified in church led to a decline in the practice of spousals (a form of marriage contract based on the exchange of vows with no church wedding) during the Elizabethan period and a corresponding decline in bridal pregnancies and illegitimacy in the early seventeenth century. While this is perhaps somewhat controversial, most historians would certainly agree that the attacks by Protestant preachers and their Puritan allies on traditional rituals and celebrations left their mark on the cultural life of early-modern England. In many areas the rhythms of communal life were disrupted, as the many seasonal festivities of the Catholic calendar, like maypole dancing on May Day and processions at Christmas, were either prohibited or fell into disuse, to be replaced by a few new religious celebrations on days of national significance, such as Elizabeth's accession-day on 17 November. At the same time, through clerical influence, there appears to have been a decline in the communal celebrations associated with the rhythms of an individual's life; by the early seventeenth century, marriage was becoming privatized as a religious rite for many families, while death too had become more of a family affair with the decline of the communal funeral wakes, which had been attacked by the clergy for their rowdiness and irreverence (Collinson 1988).

Despite its weaknesses, therefore, the late Elizabethan Church was functioning well. Apart from a minority of dissenters, the people conformed to its requirements and generally seemed satisfied with its level of pastoral care. By 1603 the Church was a relatively stable institution which reflected the social values of established householders and allowed the majority of Protestants to worship at peace in a variety of ways. It was, of course, not without its internal tensions; the Church of England was a very broad Church and relations between its most and least pious members were often strained (hence the frequent use of the term 'Puritan' as an insult) and sometimes violent – as when a young Sussex carpenter was shot in the neck and killed when assisting at the removal of a maypole from the village green at Warbleton in 1572. None the less, given the enormous upheavals taking place in religious life it is only surprising that such incidents did not escalate into wider conflict and that the Elizabethan Reformation was achieved with relatively little political unrest and without the cost of horrendous massacres or a religious war.

Elizabeth I can easily be criticized as supreme governor of the Church of England and overseer of the second English Reformation. From the time of her Royal Injunctions in the summer of 1559, her religious conservatism had put the brakes on further reform and begun to alienate the most Protestant of her subjects. Until the late 1580s, moreover, she weakened her bench of bishops by refusing to back their reforming initiatives, by encouraging the lay expropriation of ecclesiastical property and by allowing her ministers to undermine episcopal attempts to suppress the Presbyterian movement. Even in the 1590s the queen would not ratify the Lambeth Articles, approved by her own archbishop as a statement of her Church's doctrinal position. The queen seemed to be in a minority of one amongst the Protestant establishment in her religious views and consequently she can easily be blamed for the main religious controversies of the reign: the Vestiarian Controversy and political Presbyterianism

Yet Elizabeth must be given some credit for the peaceful course of the later Reformation. In the early years of the reign, her conservatism had blunted the edge of Protestant fervour and allowed many traditional features of life to survive in local communities so that the transition to Protestantism could be absorbed and tolerated the more readily by religious conservatives. Her sustained resistance to further liturgical reform also encouraged political stability, as a governmental attack on, say, prayers for the dead at funerals or the familiar rituals at baptism, which many Protestant reformers wanted, might well have provoked widespread unrest. Changes in the cultural life of a community could only be achieved gradually and with some sensitivity at a grass-roots level if they were not to have serious political repercussions.

Elizabeth I's conservatism, therefore, may well have been frustrating to her bishops and other Protestant reformers, and it may also have allowed many anomalies and abuses to continue within the Church of England. None the less, combined as it was with a degree of political flexibility, it was an important political asset and helped defuse the potential time-bomb of the second English Reformation.

References and further reading

I. Archer, *The Pursuit of Stability: Social Relations in Elizabethan London* (Cambridge, 1991)

M. Aston, *England's Iconoclasts: I. Laws Against Images* (Oxford, 1988)

J. C. H. Aveling, 'Catholic households in Yorkshire 1580–1603', *Northern History* 16 (1980)

J. Bossy, *The English Catholic Community 1570–1850* (London, 1975)

P. Christianson, 'Reformers and the Church of England under Elizabeth I and the Early Stuarts', with a comment by P. Collinson, *Journal of Ecclesiastical History* 31 (1980)

P. Collinson, *The Elizabethan Puritan Movement* (London, 1967)

P. Collinson, *The Religion of Protestants: The Church in English Society, 1559–1625* (Oxford, 1982)

P. Collinson, *English Puritanism*, Historical Association Pamphlet (London, 1983)

P. Collinson, *The Birthpangs of Protestant England* (New York, 1988)

C. Cross, *The Royal Supremacy in the Elizabethan Church* (London, 1969)

S. Doran and C. Durston, *Princes, Pastors and People: The Church and Religion in England 1529–1689* (London, 1991)

E. Duffy, *The Stripping of the Altars: Traditional Religion in England 1400–1580* (Yale, 1992)

G. R. Elton, *The Tudor Constitution*, 2nd edn (Cambridge, 1982)

R. Greaves, *Society and Religion in Elizabethan England* (Minneapolis, 1981)

C. Haigh, 'Puritan evangelism in the reign of Elizabeth I', *The English Historical Review* 92 (1977)

C. Haigh, 'From monopoly to minority: Catholicism in early modern

England', *Transactions of the Royal Historical Society*, 5th series, 31 (1981)

C. Haigh (ed.) *The Reign of Elizabeth I* (Basingstoke, 1984)

W. P. Haugaard, *Elizabeth and the English Reformation: The Struggle for a Stable Settlement of Religion* (Cambridge, 1970)

W. P. Haugaard, 'Elizabeth Tudor's Book of Devotions', *The Sixteenth Century Journal* 12 (1981)

J. A. Hilton, 'Catholicism in Elizabethan Northumberland', *Northern History* 13 (1977)

J. A. Hilton, 'The Cumbrian Catholics', *Northern History* 16 (1980)

P. Holmes, *Resistance and Compromise: The Political Thought of the Elizabethan Catholics* (Cambridge, 1982)

H. Horie, 'The Lutheran influence on the Elizabethan settlement 1558–63', *Historical Journal* 34, no. 3 (1991)

W. Hudson, *The Cambridge Connection and the Elizabethan Settlement of 1559* (Durham, NC, 1980)

M. Ingram, *Church Courts, Sex and Marriage in England, 1570–1640* (Cambridge, 1987)

N. Jones, *Faith by Statute: Parliament and the Settlement of Religion* (London, 1982)

P. Lake, 'Calvinism and the English Church 1570–1635', *Past and Present* 114 (1987)

P. Lake, *Anglicans and Puritans? Presbyterianism and English Conformist Thought from Whitgift to Hooker* (London, 1988)

J. Loach, *Parliament under the Tudors* (Oxford, 1991)

D. MacCulloch, *Suffolk and the Tudors* (Oxford, 1986)

D. MacCulloch, *The Later Reformation in England* (Basingstoke, 1990)

D. MacCulloch, 'The myth of the English Reformation', *Journal of British Studies* 30 (1991)

P. McGrath, *Papists and Puritans under Elizabeth I* (London, 1967)

P. McGrath, 'Elizabethan Catholicism: a reconsideration', *Journal of Ecclesiastical History* 35 (1984)

P. McGrath, 'The Elizabethan priests, their harbourers and helpers', *Recusant History* 19 (1989)

J. E. Neale, *Elizabeth I and her Parliaments*, vol. 1 (London, 1953)

R. O'Day, *The English Clergy: The Emergence and Consolidation of a Profession 1559–1642* (Leicester, 1979)

K. L. Parker, *The English Sabbath: A Study of Doctrine and Discipline from the Reformation to the Civil War* (Cambridge, 1987)

A. Pritchard, *Catholic Loyalism in Elizabethan England* (London, 1979)

G. Regan, *Elizabeth I* (Cambridge, 1988)

J. Spalding, *The Reformation of the Ecclesiastical Laws of England, 1552* (Missouri, 1992)

M. Spufford, *Contrasting Communities: English Villagers in the Sixteenth and Seventeenth Centuries* (Cambridge, 1974)

M. Todd, *Christian Humanism and the Puritan Social Order* (Cambridge, 1987)

K. R. Wark, *Elizabethan Recusancy in Cheshire* (Manchester, 1971)
R. Whiting, *The Blind Devotion of the People: Popular Religion and the English Reformation* (Cambridge, 1989)